GHOSTS

GHOSTS

True Tales of Eerie Encounters

Robert C. Belyk

HORSDAL & SCHUBART

Horsdal & Schubart Publishers Ltd., Victoria, BC, Canada
Distributed by The Heritage Group,
#108-17665 66A Avenue, Surrey, BC, Canada, V3S 2A7.

Cover photograph by the author; inset photo from Heritage House collection; cover design by Pat McCallum; book layout by Brenda Martin.

We acknowledge the support of The Canada Council for the Arts for our publishing program. We also acknowledge the financial support of the Government of Canada through the Book Publishing Industry Development Program (BPDIP) for our publishing activities. We also acknowledge the financial support of the Province of British Columbia through the British Columbia Arts Council.
This book is set in Goudy.

Printed and bound in Canada by Friesens, Altona, Manitoba.

National Library of Canada Cataloguing in Publication Data

Belyk, Robert C.
  Ghosts: true tales of eerie encounters / Robert C. Belyk.—
  Rev. ed.
  Previous ed. has title: Ghosts: true stories from British Columbia.
  Includes bibliographical references and index.
  ISBN 0-920663-84-2

  1. Ghosts—British Columbia. I. Title.
  BF1472.C3B44 2002   133.1'09711   C2002-911105-6

The Canada Council | Le Conseil des Arts
for the Arts | du Canada

BRITISH
COLUMBIA
ARTS COUNCIL
Supported by the Province of British Columbia

Contents

For Margaret

Preface to the Second Edition and Acknowledgments

One of the most difficult questions I'm asked is "Do you believe in ghosts?" Many readers of my ghost stories would be surprised at my answer: I have to say no. In my view, to "believe in" implies a faith that has nothing to do with proof. Thus, while I may "believe in" God, I can offer no scientific proof of God's existence. Nor would most people expect me to offer such evidence.

In the case of ghosts, though, faith should not have anything to do with these events. Instead, it is necessary to look toward the empirical evidence. And indeed there is ample proof for the existence of the paranormal.

I have made an effort to use primary sources for the accounts presented here. This has usually meant either searching through old newspaper stories and/or recording personal interviews with the witnesses involved. Many residents of this province have experienced supernatural occurrences and it is my primary purpose to tell their stories. I wish to thank everyone who kindly shared his or her experiences with me.

I would like to thank, particularly, my wife Diane whose photographic talents frequently do not receive the attention they deserve. I wish, also, to express my gratitude to Marlyn Horsdal for her support.

Preface to the First Edition

Several years ago the provincial Ministry of Tourism launched an advertising campaign using the slogan, "Super, Natural British Columbia." They were, of course, not referring to weird or bizarre happenings in the province. This was simply a play on words, drawing attention to the province's truly magnificent scenery. Yet there is a strange irony here: the slogan is also quite correct, for without doubt, British Columbia is one of Canada's most haunted provinces.

This book is a collection of some of the most interesting British Columbia ghost stories from the past and the present. These accounts have been taken from diverse sources, including British Columbia Archives files and newspaper accounts, as well as firsthand interviews. Although very different in content, these stories have one element in common: they are all claimed by their sources to be true.

Although I have included quite a few tales in this work, I realize this does not begin to scratch the surface of this province's ghost lore. If you have further information concerning any of the stories included here, or have had other ghostly encounters in British Columbia, I would like to hear from you. Please write me care of the publisher.

Robert C. Belyk

Introduction
About Ghosts and Ghost Stories

This book is about British Columbia ghosts. Although the stories presented here are limited geographically to one region, they are as diverse a collection of ghost stories as one can imagine. Unlike fictional ghost tales, which can be counted on to relieve the reader's building tension by the final page, actual stories of the supernatural are always a little unsatisfying. These stories have an unpolished feel to them; the pieces do not seem to fit together. Often, important questions are not answered. The reader is left to scratch his or her head and wonder.

Yet there is another side to this equation. These ghost stories are about real people — actual accounts of men and women who have come face to face with the world of the preternatural. For some of us, ghost stories offer nothing more than an exciting read. For others, however, these accounts point toward something more. They are a definite break with a reality that seems, on the surface at least, very well understood. These stories are a disturbing prick at our day-to-day existence — a tangible reminder that the world is a good deal more complicated than we care to acknowledge.

Ghost stories are open to widely varying interpretations. Formerly, the study of ghosts was of interest only to those delving into the field of the occult. However, in 1882, a number of prominent British academics moved toward applying the tools of science to the study of ghosts. The organization they founded was known as the Society for Psychical Research (SPR). The SPR has served as a model for psychic research throughout the world.

SO MANY GHOSTS

Those interested in Canadian ghostlore will be impressed by the sheer volume of British Columbia ghost tales. There are few such tales on the prairies (although Alberta seems to have more than the other two provinces) and only a small number in Quebec. Ontario has quite a rich collection of ghost stories, but with its far greater population, one would expect that there would be many more incidents there than in British Columbia, and this is not the case. In relation to population, only the Maritime region, with its long history of phantom ships, ghostly crews and the like, clearly has more ghost stories than British Columbia.

Interestingly, there are several theories that may account for British Columbia's large population of ghosts. First, there is the climate theory. The idea that climate plays a role in the frequency of psychic manifestations has been around for a number of years as folk wisdom. In 1963, however, the notion was given serious consideration by the distinguished anthropologist Margaret Murray, who wrote, "As [the ghost phenomenon] is known to occur in many parts of the world, it is worth noting that it is more common in moist climates than drier ones."[1] Thus, she concluded, apparitions are seen more frequently in the moister regions of Scotland and Ireland than in England with its drier climate, and similarly, the monsoon regions of India have more ghosts than the desert areas of Egypt. Like the image on a frame of photographic film, Dr. Murray believed, ghosts required the right chemical conditions to manifest themselves, and the correct conditions were somehow associated with a wet or humid atmosphere.

At first glance, British Columbia's pattern of ghostly activity seems to fit Dr. Murray's theory. If the number of ghost stories in the provincial archives will serve as a rough indicator of a region's "hauntedness," then the wet coast is far more haunted than the much drier interior. Yet there are other factors that need to be taken into account. It is also true that the most densely populated regions of the province — places where, statistically, one would expect to have more incidents reported — are also along the coast. Moreover, at least one dry area seems to have more than its share of ghosts — the old mining town of Barkerville in the Cariboo district. Thus, as far as British Columbia is concerned, it is difficult to draw any positive conclusions about the relationship between ghosts and climate.

There is a second theory, proposed by the psychic researcher T.C. Lethbridge, that may be more promising. Some time in the 1950s, while Lethbridge and his wife were walking along the English coast, they passed a small stream which ran down from the cliffs nearby. Suddenly, for no apparent reason, Lethbridge was overcome by a profound feeling of depression. As he moved away from the swift-running water the feeling of despondency lifted as abruptly as it had descended upon him. He mentioned the experience to his wife, Mina, who told him she had experienced the same changes in mood.

Later that day Mrs. Lethbridge was again overcome by a feeling of severe melancholy. She had walked up the trail to the top of the cliff where she planned to sketch the scene before her. The best spot was near a stream which eventually tumbled over the cliff to the beach below, the same stream which had so badly affected both Lethbridges earlier. She had not been working on her picture long before she was aware of a strong impulse to throw herself from the heights. Not surprisingly, Mrs. Lethbridge was very distressed by the feeling.

The couple later discovered that a man had thrown himself from the cliff — at the exact spot where Mrs. Lethbridge was sketching. The incident led Lethbridge to consider whether it was possible that the energy field generated by the moving water could somehow record psychic impressions. Certain events, he later argued, could be impressed on the water's field of energy in much the same way that sound is impressed on the magnetic field of a reel of tape.

The idea that objects "record" human events which are later "played back" to a "receiver" (a person sensitive to psychic vibrations) was not a new one. As early as 1885, Mrs. Eleanor Sidgwick, one of the pioneer members of Britain's Society for Psychical Research, postulated that apparitions were the result of something that was physically part of the structure. However, the notion that psychic impressions were associated with bodies of water was revolutionary.

Like the climate theory, Lethbridge's water-field theory appears initially quite plausible. The problem is that with the west coast's high annual rainfall, it is difficult to find any location where water is not close at hand, and the question may thus become not why there are so many ghosts, but why there are not more.

Two Kinds of Hauntings

For many years now psychic researchers have tried to come to terms with what makes one haunting case similar to or different from another, and what they have determined is that there are indeed two major kinds of ghosts: those that haunt places and those that haunt people.

Houses account for the greatest percentage of reported hauntings within the first category of ghosts. But ghosts, it seems, can haunt just about anything, from elevators to submarines. There is a particularly well-documented case of a haunted German U-boat during the First World War. Place-haunting ghosts can occupy one spot for decades, or even centuries. If all the legends are to be believed, ghosts of historical figures like Queen Mary of Scotland and Sir Walter Raleigh continue to haunt Britain's old castles.

In many instances the haunting consists of very simple acts like the sound of footsteps in the hall — repeated over and over. Often people living in haunted houses begin to take these occurrences for granted: the strange incidents become routine rather than frightening.

While the sound of phantom footsteps is one common form of this ghostly phenomenon, spectral sightings are fairly unusual.

Rarer still is speech — place-haunting ghosts seldom talk to anyone (any living person at least). Since ghosts do not have vocal cords, psychic researchers speculate that speech simulation takes a considerable amount of a ghost's energy. Ghosts have been known to try to speak, but often they succeed only in mouthing the words; very rarely is speech actually heard. The result of a ghost's use of energy may be "cold spots" — areas with drops in temperature that are frequently noted during hauntings.

On some occasions smells are associated with a haunting. Usually these odours are pleasant, but this is not always the case. Many years ago there was a case of an odour haunting the landlord of a pub in Huntingdonshire, England. Whenever the man entered the old section of his pub a singularly unpleasant smell clung to him, leaving only when he returned to the new addition. The odour was repugnant, reminding those who experienced it of a decaying carcass.

In some cases the psychic experience reported by witnesses goes beyond the perception of ghostly images, smells or sounds. In these instances it is as though a hole in the fabric of time is opened and one "sees" directly into the past. For example, a person may visit an old castle and say that he has seen the ghost of a former resident: a duke who died in 1590. When the individual is questioned it becomes clear that the incident involved more than just an ordinary haunting: the person saw not only the ghost of the 16th-century duke, but also the castle as it stood at that time. If he happened to look out a castle window, the countryside would appear not as today, but as it was four hundred years ago.

"Retrocognition," as this phenomenon is termed, is fairly common in psychical literature. One of the best-known recent examples took place in 1951 at a place not far from the beach at Dieppe, France. Two Englishwomen who were spending their summer vacation at a small hotel on the coast of France were awakened early in the morning by the sounds of airplanes, gunfire and the cries of men. The noise of battle continued for about two hours before finally fading away.

While there were other people staying at the hotel, the two women were the only witnesses and as far as they were concerned there was no question as to the sounds rising up from the beach. (They had even ventured out on the balcony of their room so they could hear better.) The hotel was located near where the infamous Dieppe Raid occurred in 1942. There, during an abortive Second World War landing, many hundreds of Canadian soldiers met their deaths. What the two women believed they heard was the sound of that ill-fated wartime operation nine years earlier.

Not all ghosts can be associated with the notion of either re-cordings or retrocognition. In many cases it seems clear that the ghostly activity is not simply a playback of the past: there is some form of intelligence behind the haunting. Often the actions of place-haunting ghosts are so purposeful they can best be described as mischievous. Their actions are usually very simple and repetitive: unscrewing some of the lights on a Christmas tree was a favourite activity of one particular ghost; turning on a tea kettle was another. For the psychic investigator, what is obvious about these ghosts is that their "tricks" seem to lack sophistication. Witnesses often describe this behaviour as child-like and some researchers speculate that it may be attention-seeking. What the ghost is really trying to say is, "Hey, notice me. I'm here too!"

The second and by far the smallest category of ghostly manifestation is the people-haunting variety — when the individual is haunted by his or her own particular spirit. There are stories of individuals being followed everywhere by mysterious shadows or even sounds. A Victoria newspaper editor, David W. Higgins, once wrote about a local man who was plagued by the sound of footsteps. Overall though, this kind of ghost seems quite rare.

A more ubiquitous personal ghost is the type which is commonly termed "crisis apparition." Crisis apparitions are different from most types of ghosts in that they may be spirits of the living rather than the dead. By definition, their appearance is always associated with intense personal crisis (and this almost inevitably involves death). A typical example would be a terminally ill patient appearing to a friend or relative (often miles away) one or two days before death. While in some cases the crisis apparition is seen after the person's death, it is never long afterwards, usually within 12 hours. The appearance of these ghosts is frequently associated with the delivery of a final personal message (either explicit or implied) to friends or loved ones. After the single visit, the apparition is usually never seen again.

A particularly nasty category of people-haunting ghost is the poltergeist. The term poltergeist means, in German, "noisy ghost," and, true to its name, the poltergeist is known for breaking cups, plates and glasses, tossing furniture about and creating a considerable fuss. For those unfortunate enough to be the focus of its malicious activities the haunting can be very physical — individuals have been pelted with stones or unceremoniously tossed from a bed onto the floor. (Rarely, though, is anyone hurt by the actions of the poltergeist.) Although modern para-psychology has come some way in understanding poltergeists, exactly what they are, and why they haunt some individuals and not others, is still a mystery.

THE OLD AND THE NEW

The reader who is unfamiliar with ghost stories of the nonfiction variety will find that these tales are rather an odd collection. Ghosts are a mixed lot. They come in just about every shape and size, and do just about anything one can imagine. This makes the organization of the material somewhat difficult, but there are several logical approaches to the subject.

For one thing, there is a definite difference between old and new British Columbia ghost stories. Many (but by no means all) of the tales from before the First World War fall into the folk-narrative category — a story told and retold for generations. Eventually some enterprising journalist hears the tale and realizes it will make a great story. The reporter then files this worn account as if it were current news. Of course, as one might imagine, the folk narrative tends to be less accurate than other ghost stories reported first- or even second-hand.

About the time of the First World War there is a change in the way newspapers presented British Columbia ghost stories. After 1918, the accounts tend to be more sophisticated and detailed; there is an increase in interviews with witnesses and a decrease in folk narratives.

GHOSTS AND SCIENCE

One clear fact that seems to apply to both place-haunting and people-haunting ghosts is that they are not bound by any known physical laws. Sometimes as wispy as mist, sometimes as solid-looking as flesh and bone, the ghostly substance is quite beyond our understanding. One of the best-documented occurrences took place in the city of Cheltenham, England, where the apparition of a woman was seen in the home of Captain F. W. Despard. Between 1882 and 1889 the ghost was observed by no fewer than 17 different people. The figure was so solid that it was mistaken for a living person on at least two different occasions, yet, when Rosina Despard, one of Captain Despard's daughters, attempted to set string traps for the apparition, it was seen to pass freely through them.

In attempting to understand ghost behaviour, it is simply impossible to reach any universal conclusions. "If one looks for reasons," according to the psychic investigator D. Scott Rogo, "psychical phenomena will soon catapult the seeker into a quagmire. Unlike the inhabitants of our securely physical world (or the domain of our physical sensations) psychical phenomena do not follow the laws of physics or perception conveniently."[2]

Moreover, because they exist almost exclusively in the "field," place-haunting ghosts stand beyond the reach of modern science. Scientists do not have the luxury of bringing them into the laboratory to study them under a microscope. When Britain's Society for Psychical Research was founded, it was believed that the enigma of ghosts and other psychic manifestations would be solved in a few years.

Introduction

Today, over a hundred years later, it must be said that while psychical research has offered some insights into the poltergeist, the traditional ghost remains almost as far removed from human understanding as ever. This does not mean that such ghosts do not exist — as will be seen in subsequent chapters, the experiences of so many credible witnesses cannot be easily dismissed — but it may be that the tools of science are entirely unsuitable for probing the nature of the paranormal. Science has aided our understanding of the material world but there is a wealth of evidence to suggest this is only part of the picture, that there are other realities which remain beyond our comprehension.

Haunted Hotels and Restaurants

ROOM CHANGE

For those who wish to enjoy the comfortable accommodation offered by the Qualicum Heritage Inn without the bother of ghosts, it is advisable to avoid one room on the fourth floor. There have been experiences elsewhere in what was once a boys' school, but this little room is certainly the most active. For many of the staff and guests, it appears that history has been captured somehow within its walls, and the scratchy vinyl of the past is sometimes played by the stylus of the present.

* * * * *

Opened in 1935, during the depth of the Great Depression, Qualicum College seemed a long way from its cultural roots. The college was created by Cambridge-educated Robert Ivan Knight. Until the Tudor-style building was completed in 1937, the school operated from a rented house in the nearby resort village of Qualicum Beach. The college was modelled after elite British public schools and although located many miles from the English heartland, it was intended to be a bulwark of the British Empire: a place where privileged classes from far-flung colonies and

1

The original wing of the Qualicum Heritage Inn was built in 1937.
(COURTESY OF D. M. BELYK)

dominions could send their sons to obtain a proper English education. Until the beginning of the Second World War, when the pitch was turned into a cadet drill ground, the most popular game on campus was cricket.

During the war, many of the young men graduating from the school joined the armed forces, and some never returned. After 1945, the world was changing and Canada's social and cultural ties to Britain had become less important. By the late 1960s, schools like Qualicum College were falling out of popular favour and many of the early faculty and staff, who had long been the foundation of the institution, were reaching retirement. At least one did not reach superannuation.

When groundskeeper Bert James failed to come down one spring day to have breakfast, college staff took notice. When he didn't turn up for lunch, janitor Alec Trumper suggested they check on him. The door to his room was locked and Trumper had to open it with a screwdriver — the groundskeeper had the habit of collecting a considerable sum in change in his bureau, so the room was always securely latched. Death had apparently taken the man suddenly, for he was sprawled on his back on the single bed, his arms raised awkwardly over his head. He died of natural causes, but coming as it did only a few months before the college finally shut its doors, the groundskeeper's passing and the close of the institution seemed tied inextricably together. It was like the end of an era.

Others who had been closely associated with the college died about the time of the school's closure in 1970. Wendy Register, the school matron much beloved by the boys, also died suddenly, shortly after her retirement.

Some of the property was sold for housing, but the school itself was remodelled to become an inn. The connection with the past, though, was not lost. One early story concerns a regular patron of the hotel who parked her car in front of the building and climbed out of the vehicle. As she did so, she happened to look toward an upstairs window. Staring back was a lone figure, a young man wearing an old-fashioned military uniform. She returned to her car and quickly drove away.

* * * * *

Because of the high staff turnover, it is often difficult to identify when the haunting began. One early non-paying guest was the spectre of a little boy. He apparently was first seen not long after the inn opened, and continues to make his presence known. When either employees or guests have approached him, he has quickly faded away. Some staff members believe that he enjoys upsetting the adults who are never able to catch him.

For many years, fourth-floor guests have been reporting distinctive noises that seem to echo up and down the hall. The noises are usually heard late at night when the hotel is otherwise quiet. Patrons have told staff that the sound is like many footsteps going along the corridor.

One of the most active haunts is certainly Room 453. It was in this room that Bert James died and many believe his spirit remains there. Housekeeping staff have reported that they have checked the room after it has been unoccupied, only to find the furnishings moved or the bed crumpled as if someone had slept on it.

In the fall of 1988, one incident frightened a guest who had come with a group of friends especially to enjoy a musician who was performing at the hotel. With no other space available, the man was put in the haunted room. It was not until early morning that the performance ended, and the man decided to forego breakfast

This is the guestroom that is believed to be haunted by
the college's former groundskeeper.
(COURTESY OF D. M. BELYK)

and sleep in. As he later told hotel employees, he was lying awake when he heard the sound of the door opening. Suddenly the covers were stripped from him and a voice told him to get down to breakfast. In minutes, he was dressed and in the dining room.

One particularly strange event took place in 1988 when Devon Andrew accompanied her husband, Adrian, who was attending a trade show in Qualicum. Adrian had been to the area many times, and the Qualicum Heritage Inn was his favourite stopover. They took a room in the original structure — two wings have been added to the building since its conversion to an inn — and retired about 11 PM. A short time later Devon entered a state between wakefulness and sleep. She had experienced sleepwalking episodes before but nothing like the one that occurred this night. In her altered state of consciousness, she became convinced that her husband was missing somewhere in the hotel and went to search for him. She had moved through most of the corridors of the hotel before her husband was called to the night desk to retrieve his sleepwalking wife at 3 AM.

When she awoke in the morning, Devon recalled a vivid dream from the night before; until Adrian mentioned he had been summoned to the front desk, however, she had no idea she had been sleepwalking. Remarkably, her memory of the stairways, corridors, rooms and even the roof remained clear. Devon recalled trying the doors along the fourth-floor corridor:

> Somewhere in the hallway a small door opened on my left and a woman was standing there. I could see past her into the room. It was old and tiny. There was a small single bed butted up to the wall on one side and [on the] other was a sink, mirror and a small door I thought led to a small bathroom of sorts. The ceiling was sloped, almost as if the room was into the eaves of the building. [The occupant] was a bit irate (who wouldn't be after being woken up in the night!!!).[1]

Devon continued in her apparently trance-like state to the stairway that led to the third floor. "I started to venture down [the long hallway] when a small boy of six or seven suddenly appeared walking away from me. He turned to look at me over his left shoulder and seemed to disappear through a door on the left side of the hallway."

Later that day, when the couple visited hotel executive Linda Bishop to apologize for the disturbance the previous night, Devon related her dream. Together, the three retraced her steps. As they proceeded through the building, Linda pointed out a room with no numbers on the door. She explained that it did have a number, but that it was small and rarely occupied by guests.

"Let me tell you the layout of the room," Devon said before Linda could open the door. And she did, "detail for detail, including a small bed against the wall, the sink, the small door to a tiny bathroom and the sloping ceiling."

Linda then explained to the couple that this was Room 459, known as the "ghost room." The reason that there were no numbers on the door was that the numerals kept disappearing. (Later, when the room number was changed from 459 to 453, the metal numbers finally remained in place.) Over the years, many other incidents have been associated with this tiny space.

How could Devon have known the interior of the room? The obvious answer was that she had seen the inside when the female guest opened the door. But the hotel was not completely booked and the room had not been taken. It should have been unoccupied. If the woman was a ghost, though, why was she in the room so long occupied by Bert James?

One floor down, the three people walked along the corridor where Devon had seen the small boy. She described how he disappeared through the door. It had been Room 341, that of Robert Ivan Knight, the school's headmaster.

Devon's story, although fascinating, is only one of the strange incidents that have taken place at the Qualicum Heritage Inn. In the fall of 1998, Ruth Hutchinson and her son Michael were guests of the hotel. The exceptional service and charming ambience made it a pleasant place to spend a quiet time away from the usual grind of daily life and they enjoyed the beauty of the natural setting.

Michael Hutchinson, who liked a large room with an ocean view, booked accommodation on the fourth floor, while Ruth took a room on the third. Michael was in his room shaving when the lights flickered off and on several times. Then the television set suddenly came on. Michael turned it off, but it came on again. In Ruth's room on the third floor, nothing unusual happened and Michael, with the exception of this one incident, enjoyed a pleasant and relaxing stay.

During the spring of the next year, Ruth and Michael decided to spend another few days at the inn. On this occasion it was not possible for Ruth to book her usual third-floor room, so she accepted a bright and charming fourth-floor room. The day of her arrival was quiet, and Ruth enjoyed the spring flowers that could be seen in the garden below her window. Michael had taken his usual room farther down the corridor on the opposite side of the hall.

After a restful night, Ruth decided to spend part of the day in her room. She lay on her bed reading her book. Neither the radio nor the television was turned on. As she recalled later:

> For the next half-hour I enjoyed some quiet solitary time. Then from the wall behind me I heard what resembled an adolescent boy's muffled crying. He appeared to be in physical pain. For a couple of minutes I listened carefully, as I didn't want to disturb what may have been a family dispute. As the crying became more clear and increased in volume I became aware of several other muffled voices. There was also an older female voice that appeared to be trying to soothe the injured youth.[2]

The sound filtering from the other room continued for three or four minutes with the other voices fading until all that remained was that of the boy and the older woman. As the whimpering began to subside, Ruth arose and went into the hallway, expecting to be able to tell from which room the sound was coming. To her astonishment, she could hear neither the adolescent nor the woman. When she returned to her room, the sounds had ceased.

Unsure whether she had happened to hear a family quarrel or voices from beyond this earthly realm, Ruth again picked up her book. She had no opportunity to begin before she was aware of a muffled chanting from somewhere nearby. The words made no sense, but the speech had a rhythmic flow. The chanting changed from time to time. Occasionally all the voices were speaking in unison while at other times only a single voice kept the rhythm. To Ruth's growing horror, the volume of the voices was increasing. Even more frightening, she was sure the sound was coming from the next room. "I got off the bed and placed my ear to the wall. Immediately the chanting stopped."

It didn't resume again but by now Ruth was very upset. She left the lights on in her room and switched on the television. She suddenly felt exposed to something unseen but nonetheless present. "I would not even run a shower," she recalled later.

The next morning they were to leave and Ruth dressed for the drive to her home. She was sitting at the vanity table when suddenly she heard a long, continuous moan from the space between the two beds. "I was so startled that I immediately opened the door to the hallway." When Michael arrived, Ruth told him of her experiences. Rather than doubting his mother, Michael explained that on previous visits he had heard what appeared to be the sound of adolescents running in the hall and doors slamming.

Before leaving, Ruth and Michael spoke with two chambermaids working on the fourth floor:

> I said I'd had a terrible night and I was quite upset from it all. I simply stated that strange things were happening in my room. The chambermaids informed us that a previous party had heard piano music and then later, singing from the same room. We were told also that it wasn't uncommon, as other people had complained of similar events. For me it was a relief to have confirmed that I wasn't the only one and hadn't imagined the entire experience.

Although the identity of the young person Ruth heard isn't known, many believe the older female voice to be that of Wendy

Register, the school matron. It was not uncommon for boys separated from their friends and families to be inconsolable and Wendy did much to ease their adaptation to Qualicum College life.

The next month Ruth and Michael had an opportunity to spend another weekend at the inn. After her previous experiences, Ruth made sure to book her usual room on the third floor. The next day Ruth met Michael at his room because she wanted to see the ocean view from that angle. Mother and son were planning to enjoy a pleasant lunch in the dining room, but Michael wasn't ready and Ruth decided she would go on ahead:

> I descended the long narrow staircase back to the third floor. Nearing the third step [above] the landing I heard a man's heavy pounding footsteps coming from behind me. As I felt a presence I moved to one side to allow the guest to pass as the person sounded in a hurry. To my shock when I turned around the staircase behind me was empty. In fear [and] without thinking I jumped the three steps to the landing and ran for safety through the door.

* * * * *

Another entity seems to haunt the hotel lobby and restaurant area. In 1995, server Jeanie Mathieson arrived to begin the early shift. The area where the coffee was prepared was at the back of a small room off the hall between the kitchen and the restaurant. Before turning the machine on, Jeanie added water to the reservoir, put the grounds into the cone containing the drip filter and then returned the plastic cassette to its slot in the coffee maker. All that was required was to wait a few minutes for the coffee to drip through the filter. Meanwhile, she turned her attention to the supply table at the front of the area. She restocked the condiment bottles and put out the small cream containers for the coffee.

As Jeanie went about her tasks, she heard a crash from behind her — where the coffee was being prepared. She rushed to the spot and found the plastic cassette lying about six or seven feet from the coffee maker. The grounds were strewn across the floor.

Since the cassette fit securely in its slot in the coffee machine, Jeanie was puzzled. For the server who had much to do before the arrival of the first customers, the act seemed like a mischievous prank.

Two years later, when Jeanie was again working the early shift, she heard another crash from the coffee area. As before, she found the filter cassette across the room and the coffee grounds again strewn over the floor. Jeanie, who was particularly busy that morning, was more annoyed than frightened. "Listen, you little beggar," she said. "I don't have time for this. Get the heck out of here."[3] Since then, there have been no further incidents with the coffee machine.

In 1998, Joey Legate worked at the front desk of the hotel. During evening shifts, she had many encounters with the ghost she called "Buddy" who seemed to enjoy interfering with the electrical equipment.

One telephone line was dedicated for credit approval from the major card companies. Its only other use was as the front-desk house phone. "Obviously," Joey realized, "if someone were using the line, I would know."[4] Yet frequently during the seven months she worked at the inn, Joey noticed that the line produced a busy signal. No light on the switchboard was lit to indicate the line was engaged, but when she picked up the telephone she heard the characteristic buzzing sound. At first Joey was perplexed, but after hearing some of the stories about the hotel, she began to believe that Buddy was simply trying to make his presence known. As she recalled:

> I could not just think, "I wish Buddy would get off the phone!" I would have to ask out loud. "Buddy — please give me 15 minutes to get these approvals done." I would have to wait five to ten minutes, but the line would be clear — and only for the time I asked for. I would chastise Buddy for being on the phone so long, and often suggested he wait until the next night to get back on the line. He did what I asked!

Buddy also appears to have had an influence on the printer at the front desk, which frequently failed to work, but his greatest interest was the phone line. Although the apparent psychic activity at the desk has been less frequent lately, the office equipment sometimes seems to be controlled by unseen forces. One of the mysteries that puzzle many of the employees of Qualicum Heritage Inn is this: who is Buddy calling?

LADY CHURCHILL AND BRADY

Although the ghosts are from a bygone era, the haunting of the Bedford Regency, a 44-room upscale hotel on Government Street in Victoria, is comparatively recent. The first spirit was seen in the 1980s when the city's downtown core was undergoing extensive renovations, and the entity has remained there since the hotel was opened in 1994. And he is not the only unregistered guest. The ghost of a young woman also haunts the Bedford Regency.

While the identities of the ghosts remain a mystery, the hotel staff call them "Lady Churchill" and "Brady." Janitor Lucy Wong's first experience with Brady happened while she was employed to clean up the construction site. She and another worker were in the lobby when they heard a noise coming from the direction of the staircase. "We didn't see the person but we saw his shadow. He wore a derby hat and was coming down."[5]

Some time later, Lady Churchill made her presence known. While the details of the sighting have been mostly lost, she was described as wearing a pretty, old-fashioned yellow dress.

Like Brady, Lady Churchill is often seen in silhouette. During the summer of 2000, desk clerk Dan Hooper was on duty one morning when a guest approached. The man asked if the hotel was haunted. When Hooper replied that some people believed so, the man said, "Yeah, I saw a ghost in my room last night."[6]

Apparently he had awakened to see a woman's shadow standing by the fireplace on the wall opposite his bed. She was wearing a flared dress in the style of the late 19th century. When he sat up, the shape suddenly disappeared.

Staff and guests have commented on the perfume that sometimes hangs in the air, particularly on the fourth floor. In

October 2000, a guest decided to go out while her husband spent the evening at the hotel. When she returned she was struck by the scent of very heavy cologne that clung to the area outside her room. Expecting to find a visitor, she slipped her key into the lock and pushed open the door. However, the only person in the room was her husband, sitting quietly in a chair reading a newspaper.

Several incidents have taken place in the basement. During the renovations, Lucy Wong was cleaning the basement when she suddenly felt a sharp tap on her shoulder. She looked around but no one was there. Some months later another employee was cleaning a large mirror in the basement when she caught a glimpse of a man standing behind her. She quickly turned around, but the room was vacant.

During restorations, Victoria's Bedford Regency Hotel was the site of several hauntings. (COURTESY OF D. M. BELYK)

Not all incidents are typical of a haunting. Dan Hooper witnessed an occurrence in 1999, when only he and another desk clerk were on duty. During the evening they registered a couple and the pair took their own luggage to their room. The man found that he couldn't unlock the door. All the rooms are secured by a deadbolt that can only be locked from inside the room. In this case there was an adjoining room and Hooper reasoned that the last occupant had left via the connecting room. Hooper opened the door and bolted the inside adjoining door. After they put their luggage away, the couple passed the desk on their way to dinner and returned a couple of hours later. Hooper recalled, "They went to go in their room and it was deadbolted again. And there was just me and the other person working and neither of us went up and locked the door. And no one could get in the room so it had to be locked from the inside."

There has been much speculation about whether Lady Churchill and Brady inhabit only the Bedford Regency Hotel or whether they range farther afield to other haunts in Victoria's downtown core.

THE GUEST AT TABLE 15

Few of Victoria's older hotels seem to escape at least one presence, and Victoria's Cherry Bank Hotel has two resident ghosts. The 26-room hotel on Burdett Avenue was built in 1897 for James Graham Brown and his family. Brown was the architect who designed Victoria's St. Andrew's Presbyterian Church at the corner of Douglas and Courtney.

The Brown family's house was given the name "Cherry Bank" because it was set at the edge of an orchard. In 1906 a new wing was added to accommodate the expanding family but by 1912, the children had reached adulthood and moved away, and rooms were let to boarders. By 1933, the house had changed hands several times and in the 1940s it was converted into a small hotel. The current proprietor, David Bowman, has operated the hotel since 1984.

When the ghostly happenings began at the Cherry Bank Hotel isn't known, but the management has long had difficulty keeping a night janitor. Many employees complained of unexplained knocks and strange incidents. Doors that were firmly closed and locked would be found open; windows would be heard to slam.

In 1977 one janitor complained that while he was in the middle of cleaning, the vacuum cleaner would suddenly quit. Even when the machine was close to an outlet, and he was not putting pressure on the cord, the plug would be found pulled out from the socket. This would occur repeatedly during his shift.

In the mid-1990s, one janitor reported entering a washroom to find that the sink and counter were covered with a thick layer of dust. It did not appear to be thrown, but spread evenly as if the dust had collected over many years.

* * * * *

One of the long-time permanent residents of the hotel was Mrs. Houston (a pseudonym) who had a room on the first floor near the front entrance. An elderly lady, she was experiencing the effects of age and was almost completely blind. During her years at the hotel, she established a routine whereby she entered the dining room when it opened at five o'clock and, due to her limited eyesight, she would pace the distance to her usual place at Table 15. Often she began with a glass of sherry and followed it with the sparerib entrée.

By 1975, Mrs. Houston was becoming increasingly difficult to manage, and it was clear that she needed more care than the hotel could provide. After the manager spoke with the woman's nephew, arrangements were made for her transfer to a nursing home. Although declining in health, Mrs. Houston didn't wish to leave her room at the Cherry Bank, since it had been her home for some years. Not long after her move, the hotel staff received news that she had died.

Shortly after Mrs. Houston's room became vacant, the hotel decided to convert it, with the adjacent alcove, into a banquet facility that could be used for private events. In it were one long table and three or four small tables which could accommodate about 40 people in all. The new room had a public entrance, which could be locked until the area was to be used, as well as an open serving connection to the kitchen.

In 1987 a young woman began work at the hotel as a server. The banquet table and several of the smaller tables had been booked for that evening and she was asked to arrange the place settings. She obtained the place mats, tumblers, sideplates and other items from the kitchen and returned by the staff entrance. When she pushed the door open, she discovered that the three chandeliers that lit the banquet room had been turned off and the room was in darkness. Only a few minutes earlier, when she had inspected the room, it had been brightly illuminated. Now with the lights off, she had to search for the switch.

Once the lights were on again, she began setting the tables until she realized she did not have everything she needed. She went quickly to the kitchen and found the items. When she returned, the room was again in darkness.

Since she was aware that no other person had entered through the kitchen, the only explanation seemed to be that someone had come through the public entrance to play a prank on her. As in many jobs, it was not uncommon for servers to play practical jokes on new employees. As she quickly realized, though, this explanation didn't hold. The public entrance was locked from the inside and no one could open it unless they were in the banquet room.

Puzzled, the server went to the main dining room where she found the hostess. Together the women returned to the banquet room, which was once again in darkness. When the lights were turned on, to their surprise the place settings for one of the smaller tables had been removed and placed neatly on the floor. The table was one of several in the area that had once been Mrs. Houston's room.

The hostess concluded that someone must be hiding in one of the washrooms, but when she checked them both were empty. Now upset by the happenings, the server returned to the kitchen and obtained the final items needed to prepare the room. When she returned, the lights had been turned off again and when she switched them on once more, the table's place settings had been removed again. This time they were not on the floor, but placed on each chair seat. According to assistant manager Barbara Filby who was there at the time, the new server immediately "took her apron off and quit."[7]

After Mrs. Houston's death a number of patrons who were seated at her former table complained of feeling uncomfortable. Some have felt a cold draft. "A guest said he felt someone was looking over his shoulder and his hair was standing on end. One couple were surprised the small brass accent lamp moved across the table on its own. They immediately asked for another table. It became one of those tables that you would have to wait until the room was completely full before you used it."

In the late 1990s, two young men interested in the subject of Victoria's ghosts as a film-school project approached Barbara Filby and asked to be seated at Table 15 while they interviewed her. "I was talking," she recalled, "and all of a sudden there was this crash

It is said that one of the ghosts of the Cherry Bank Hotel does not want to give up her seat at Table 15. (COURTESY OF D. M. BELYK)

behind the bar. We got up and looked, but nothing was there to show that something happened. The crash was loud like something fell on the floor, but there was nothing there."

* * * * *

The ghosts that haunt the Cherry Bank Hotel are rarely seen. Some time ago a woman with white hair and a long dark dress was seen by the night watchman. When or where this took place isn't known. More recently a night staff person saw a little blond girl standing by Room 4. The man stood watching her until she began running down the hall. Like the sighting of the woman, the details concerning the apparition of the little girl remain vague.

Room 4 has long been referred to as the haunted room. Many visitors seem to find spending a night in the same room as a ghost or ghosts exciting, and ask to spend the night there. One such couple spent a peaceful night but awoke to find the door to the bathroom removed from its hinges.

Other odd occurrences have taken place at the hotel. Opposite the bar in the lounge there was an old pay phone. When the telephone rang, the bartender had to stop whatever he or she was doing and come out from behind the bar to answer it. To end the inconvenience, an old-fashioned black cradle telephone was installed at the bar in the early 1980s; this permitted the bartender to answer the pay phone using the cradle phone. While long-time employee Kathy found the phone handy, the instrument had one annoying quirk. In the morning when Kathy was alone, setting up the bar for the day, the receiver would jump off the hook and fall to the counter. Often she was not near the phone, so it was impossible for her to find a logical reason for this action, which always occurred when no one else was around.

When Kathy finally mentioned the strange behaviour of the receiver, other staff members clearly didn't believe her and found the story amusing. Barbara Filby also had difficulty believing that the phone was able to launch itself into the air. However, one day after work Filby was met at the hotel by her husband and several friends. They were sitting at the end of the bar chatting with Kathy, who was engrossed in telling a story while she delivered drinks. As she walked past the telephone the receiver suddenly jumped high into the air. With those sitting at the bar looking on in amazement, "Kathy didn't stop, she didn't change her stride. She caught it in mid-air and hung it up as if it never happened." For Kathy the incidents with the phone had become so commonplace that her actions were automatic. Those who had witnessed this event were amazed. "Nobody until then had believed her. Well, all of a sudden we were believers."

THE SPIRITS OF "OLDE ENGLAND"

Against common wisdom, it is not always the building that is haunted. As has been noted elsewhere, entities are often connected with the furnishings rather than the structures themselves. In the case of the Olde England Inn, on Lampson Street, Esquimalt, it seems that the ghosts are connected with the vast assortment of antique furnishings that complement its architecture.

* * * * *

Designed by the well-known Victoria architect Samuel Maclure, "Rosemead" was completed for the T. H. Slater family in 1909. Maclure's Tudor houses were reminiscent of the large, half-timbered manors of rural England. Rosemead remained the Slater family residence until 1939, when it was turned into an officers' mess. Wing Commander Samuel Lane, recently of the Royal Air Force, purchased the house in 1946 and turned it into a hotel. Lane, who had been in the antiques business before the war, outfitted his inn with period furniture purchased in Britain. Some of the larger rooms had individual fireplaces and antique canopy beds. Lane added a number of new features to the property including an accurate replica of Anne Hathaway's cottage.

Because of the high staff turnover that typifies the business, it is difficult to find first-hand witnesses to the early occurrences at the hotel. The stories, though, have been passed down over the years. One tale is set in the Elizabethan Room with its beautiful 16th-century carved-oak bed. About 2 AM, the night clerk was briefly away from his desk and when he returned, he was met by the single occupant of the Elizabethan Room. The woman, who was still

Some believe that the actual structures of the Olde England Inn complex are not haunted. The ghosts, instead, are closely connected to the room furnishings imported from Europe. (COURTESY OF D. M. BELYK)

dressed in her nightclothes, was very upset and it took several minutes before she was sufficiently composed to tell her story.

She said that she had gone to bed earlier that evening and had awakened a few minutes before two in the morning with the feeling that she was not alone in the room. Somebody was there with her. As her eyes adjusted to the light, she was aware of a bearded man, whom she later described as wearing old-fashioned clothing, floating above her. She fled from the room. The guest, however, remained the only witness to the occurrence. When the clerk and security staff investigated, there was no intruder in the room.

The King of Portugal Room contains a bed that was reputedly once occupied by the Portuguese monarch at the beginning of the 19th century. Like the other theme suites, this deluxe accommodation is popular with people celebrating their wedding or anniversary. An American couple, who had been married in Victoria, returned to the city to celebrate their 15th wedding anniversary. They had reserved the King of Portugal Room and planned to spend a romantic evening in front of the fire. Beforehand, the man decided to remain in the room and take a relaxing bath while his wife visited friends in the city. After his wife left, he locked the door from the inside and proceeded to the bathroom. Some time later, he stepped out of the tub, towelled off and then, realizing that he did not have fresh clothes, walked into the outer room. To his amazement, he was not alone, for sitting on the hearth before the fireplace was an attractive young woman. She had long blond hair that tumbled over the nightdress she was wearing.

Embarrassed, the man quickly reentered the bathroom to drape himself in a towel. When he returned, however, the person who had been sitting on the hearth was gone. Perplexed, he searched the room. There was no outside balcony on which to escape and the man noted that the hallway door remained latched. Since he did not wish the romantic evening with his wife to be shared with a ghost, he requested a room change. The blond woman has been seen on other occasions in the King of Portugal Room, but the details of those sightings have been lost.

Not all the happenings at the Olde England Inn are associated with the theme suites. In September 2001, clerk Will Wilburn was working the night shift at the front desk of the hotel when he suddenly heard a woman's voice drifting down from the second-floor balcony. She was singing an aria, a piece that could almost be described as "haunting," Wilburn recalled. "It made the hair stand up on my arm."[8] When he climbed the stairs, the music stopped abruptly. Wilburn heard the same beautiful voice in the same song late one night several months later, but he has not heard it since.

Built in 1956, and furnished with antiques from the 16th and 17th centuries, Anne Hathaway's Cottage is another location with its share of ghosts. Tour guide Gerald Parish has noted that many of the guides feel a hostile presence in one of the upstairs bedrooms. The feeling was so strong for one guide that she refused to remain in the house after dusk. There may have been good reason. The bartenders and waiters who frequently work late and pass the cottage on their way to the staff parking lot have caught glimpses of a woman in the upstairs window. Since the cottage is well secured at this time, it would be impossible for any living person to gain entry without triggering the alarms. There is a general feeling among the staff that this is not a place to linger at night.

While Parish has not seen the woman at the window, a period Bible opened to a particular page in a display case is sometimes turned to a different page. Because of its age and value, the Bible is rarely handled by anyone. He also has seen an ornately carved 16th-century chair, which is tipped backward against the wall (to discourage use), returned to its upright position when he arrives the next morning. This is a ghost who apparently wants everything in its proper place.

"HELPING OUT" IN THE KITCHEN

"I never really believed in ghosts," Lloyd Gorgerson said, "but there is something here."[9] As the co-owner of Pounders Restaurant on Yates Street, Gorgerson was commenting on the strange events that he and his staff had experienced at the restaurant.

The location has a long and colourful history for, during the early years of the rush for gold in British Columbia, Yates Street was one of the busiest thoroughfares in Victoria. The block on Yates between Wharf and Langley streets featured many seedy inns. One was the Great American Hotel, which no doubt was the scene of much celebration on American Independence Day, for many of the prospectors were from the United States.

At the end of the 19th century, the wooden structure burned, and a brick building was put up in its place. Since then it has served as an office, storehouse, opium den, brothel and finally a warehouse before it became part of Victoria's urban redevelopment. The building was restored and new businesses, including a hair salon and Pounders Restaurant, were opened.

Proprietor Gorgerson first became aware that something strange was happening at his restaurant when he restored the mezzanine floor that had been removed many years earlier. On a number of occasions, customers have claimed to feel the presence of a ghost in the dining area. One long-time patron was surprised to feel a prickly sensation as the hair stood up on the back of his neck. Although nothing was seen, the man told Gorgerson that he knew the ghost was standing behind his chair. Sometimes staff members were aware of footsteps pacing on the mezzanine and when anyone went upstairs to investigate, the footsteps stopped abruptly. There was never anything to be seen.

One particular noise, though, has been more disturbing. It sounds as if someone is pounding on the bathroom door. While the noise sometimes echoes from the men's lavatory, it is also heard in the direction of the women's facility. "There is no way the wind can do it," Gorgerson observed, "because both the women's and the men's rooms have heavy door closures to keep them shut." Like the mysterious footsteps, the thumping cannot be explained by the staff.

Who is it that haunts Pounders? There may be one clue. In the early 1990s, one of the staff from the hair salon next door heard what she believed was a noise coming from Pounders. Given the hour, the staff would be cleaning up in preparation for the next day and the hairdresser thought it was an opportunity to get a cup of coffee before the restaurant closed. However, when she pulled on the door to the restaurant it was locked. To her surprise, when she peered in she saw a young woman sitting on the stairway to the mezzanine floor. She was dressed in a long, off-white gown with frills and buttons running up the front. The two stared at each other for several moments before the woman turned and walked up the stairs. When she reached the top she simply disappeared.

There is nothing malevolent about the ghost, although she is sometimes mischievous. The restaurant décor includes a carriage lamp fixed securely to a post. Gorgerson's first task in the morning when he arrives at work is to turn on the lights and do a "walk through" to ensure everything is in order. On his initial check, the carriage lamp is in its upright position. When he returns to the dining room later, the lamp is sometimes turned sideways. Considerable effort is needed to change its position, and, before the arrival of the other staff, Gorgerson is the only person there.

According to Gorgerson, the ghost doesn't confine her activities to the dining room: "She loves to play with my stove, to turn the burners up or down. In some cases she's turned them off when I've forgotten to do it. Or I guess if she's annoyed with me, she'll turn a burner right up so when I come to cook a meal it burns." Sometimes staff will go to the kitchen and find crockery that is normally stored on a high shelf placed on the tiled floor. If any pieces had fallen they would have been smashed, but there is never anything broken.

In September 2000, the ghost apparently made her displeasure known when Gorgerson hired a man as a casual employee. That day, "all kinds of weird things were going on: strange noises that sounded like rice being thrown against the wall. I'd come around and look and there's nobody there. One time all the burners were turned up right on high." After the man left, the ghost seemed to return to her usual self.

Two months later, one of the servers working in the dining room caught a glimpse of someone in white entering through the back door. She thought it was the chef, who wears a white jacket, but when she went into the kitchen, no one was there. Only on one occasion has Gorgerson seen something strange. He was washing vegetables in the sink when he witnessed a small black object, about the size of a credit card, fall from an upper shelf onto the preparation table, and strike with a distinct clatter. Engrossed in his work he paid the incident little notice. Several minutes later when he had time to retrieve the fallen item, he was surprised to discover that there was nothing on the table. Whatever had fallen had apparently disappeared.

Gorgerson notes that the entity became active after the restoration of the mezzanine floor and it is possible that she was one of the women who earned her living at the brothel. Because many ghosts apparently haunt the downtown core and surrounding area, it is certainly possible that the restaurant is not the only building that she haunts. However, she does seem to have a firm bond with the restaurant.

A Haunted Heritage

I n 1905 the city of Vancouver was taking its place as one of Canada's most important cities. For the city's many real estate speculators, the Burnaby valley to the east seemed to be a potential gold mine. The British Columbia Electric Railway was already committed to opening a tramline from Vancouver to New Westminster and with transportation ensured, many Vancouver real estate men and their friends saw the Deer Lake corridor as prime development property. This land was subdivided into large, fully serviced lots that commanded high prices.

To ensure that the lots attracted the "right" people, the houses to be built had to be appraised at $8,000. Within a few years some of the lots were sold at lower than market prices to wealthy friends and associates of the developers, to show that the Deer Lake project attracted the city's new moneyed class.

The first lots were put on the open market in 1911, but by then the unbridled real estate expansion was nearing its end and in the autumn of 1912, the market collapsed. For the new owners of the property around Deer Lake, losses were not confined to the values of their own estates. Some were major players in the Vancouver market and the crash brought them close to financial disaster. By 1913, the dream of an extensive upper-scale community had died. Some owners were unable to maintain their houses and these dwellings fell into disrepair. Hundreds of the acres that the developers had not sold became municipal lands when the owners were unable to pay the taxes. Other estates were bought at "fire sale" prices and over the years, the residences around Burnaby Lake frequently changed hands.

In the 1960s and 1970s, Burnaby purchased several of the houses in recognition of their importance as heritage sites. With the houses came a large number of resident ghosts. While Fairacres is indeed the best-documented haunting, at least two other houses within the heritage complex have been the focus of strange happenings.

ANDERSON HOUSE

Anderson House is considerably smaller and lacks the grand façades of either the Ceperley or Mathers mansions. It has no majestic towers or long, covered balconies, but its simple Arts and Crafts design with half-timbered Tudor gables remains pleasing to the eye. The house was built for Robert and Elizabeth Anderson in 1912. The Andersons, however, lost interest in the estate after their son was killed in the First World War. Subsequently, the dwelling was owned by a succession of people prior to its purchase about 1940 by Benedictine monks from the Mount Angel Seminary of Oregon. They also purchased Fairacres and Mathers House, to function as the Seminary of Christ the King. Fairacres served as the priory while Mathers House accommodated the first-year seminary students; Anderson House was home to the second-year students as well as Grey Nuns from Ontario who acted as support people for the seminary. The nuns lived on the second floor above the seminary students.

When the order moved to Mission, the Deer Lake property was sold to private owners and was eventually bought by Burnaby Council. Anderson House was then converted to offices for employees of that city's cultural programs.

Donna Redlick has been a programmer with the Burnaby Cultural Affairs Department since 1990. Whenever she went

The ghost of Anderson House has a "soft spot" for music of the big-band era.
(COURTESY OF D. M. BELYK)

to her office on the second floor of Anderson House, she would begin to sing and hum tunes from the 1930s and 1940s. It was music with which Donna was unfamiliar, but she often vocalized anyway. Other colleagues heard classical music that was only faintly audible.

Not all the activities at Anderson House were so benign. In May 1999, Ruth Hoyem, an arts programmer, was working late at the Shadbolt Centre, where most of the scheduled projects take place. She finished about 10 AM and walked the short distance to Anderson House to fill out her time slip. The security system requires a coded entry, and Ruth punched in the numbers. After entering, she pulled the latch shut and the door locked automatically.

After Ruth had gone upstairs, she heard the latch close again. Moments later footsteps came up the stairs. "I thought maybe it was the custodian or somebody else who had come into the building, but there was nobody else there."[1]

A few minutes later she walked down to the main floor. Returning upstairs, she sat again at her desk. She recalled, "I heard the same sound of the coded door opening and shutting, and also the sound of somebody walking up the stairway." The sound disappeared before it reached the second floor. After that, as Ruth observed, "I was pleased to leave."

Donna Redlick had similar experiences:

> Sometimes I would work late into the evening when nobody else would be there. Sometimes I would just get the sensation that someone was there and a couple of times I would hear footsteps coming up the stairs.[2]

Donna waited for the person to appear on the second floor, but no one reached the top of the steps. She walked over to the stair rail and called down, "Hello, is anybody there? Is that the custodian?" There was no answer. "There were probably two or three occasions," Donna recalled, "when I just got the heck out of there because I was shaken up." She recalls one morning in 2001, when the intense smell of lavender seemed to be as thick as fog in Anderson House. Lavender has long been associated with a ghostly presence, including the ghost or ghosts who haunt Fairacres.

JAMES COWAN THEATRE

James Cowan Theatre was built by the Benedictines in the early 1950s as a gymnasium and was later converted into Burnaby's civic theatre. When the building was renovated as part of the heritage project, many unusual occurrences were observed. A faucet in one of the bathrooms has been seen many times to turn itself on and off. The jingling of keys is also heard at night, when the building should be unoccupied except for the cleaning staff.

There is also an apparition: that of a young woman walking along the hallway. She has long hair that curls over what is apparently a nightgown. While the ghost seems to be without malice, she has frightened the custodians who work in the theatre. Her identity and why she has chosen such an odd location to haunt remain a mystery.

MATHERS HOUSE

One of the Burnaby Lake mansions that went beyond traditional Edwardian architecture was the house of William and Mary Mathers. While not quite to the scale of Fairacres, Mathers House was an impressive dwelling in its day. The house is in the Romanesque Revival style with a prominent tower. Guests entered through a two-storey turret complete with battlements. Inside, long narrow arched windows cast light down on the entrance hall. The ornate plaster of the lobby and the fine hardwood decorating the turret room defined the quality of the residence.

Finished in 1913, the house remained in the Mathers family until William's death in 1935. Mathers House was purchased by the previously mentioned Benedictine order in 1939 and became part of the Seminary of Christ the King.

William Franklin Wolsey, also known as "Archbishop John I," purchased the estate in 1954 for use by his sect, the Canadian Temple of the More Abundant Life. The organization was formally called the Canadian Temple of the Universal Foundation of More Abundant Life.

In 1959, the Vancouver *Sun* exposed Wolsey as a convicted bigamist who had a string of extortion and wife-beating charges throughout the eastern United States. Archbishop John, the newspaper revealed, had been consecrated in London in the year 1955 by Archbishop Percival Nicholson, Primate of the Ancient Catholic Church (and former waiter at London's Savoy Hotel). Moreover, the impressive degrees which Wolsey so proudly displayed were shown to be entirely bogus — purchased from British and American degree mills.

After years of scandal that finally left the sect in ruin, the building was once more on the market. During their time, the temple had damaged much of the interior of the house, including the kitchen, tower and stairway. For a short time the building was used as a preschool, but in 1971 Burnaby Council purchased it as the home of that city's pottery guild and for employee offices.

For some employees who worked at Mathers House, it was more than simply the building's dilapidated condition that was unsettling. One of the custodial staff complained that on several occasions he had entered the house to find the toys, once used by the preschool and stored neatly in the turret, tossed around the room. The custodian was less concerned about the presence of a ghost than the extra effort it took to clean up the mess.

In 1978, four potters planned to spend the night in the house to finish firing their work. All were aware of the ghost stories associated with the building, and as a result, they had requested that the door leading from the clay room to the rest of the house be closed off. As they readied their pots for firing, the women heard a disturbance on the other side of the door — the sound of

One of the ghosts of Mathers House has a malevolent nature. The spirit appears to dislike children. (COURTESY OF D. M. BELYK)

objects striking the walls and floor in the other room. Although upset by the experience, they continued working until the early hours of the morning. As they left by the side entrance and walked around the corner, they were struck by a frightening sight. Through the windows of one of the large rooms at the front, they saw a mass of eerie lights that appeared and disappeared through the ebb and flow of a mist. There was no doubt in anyone's mind that the source was supernatural. What they had seen was probably connected to the earlier disturbances in the tower, but who or what it was could not be explained. As far as the employees at Mathers House were concerned, this was a malicious presence.

There is a story that soon after Mathers House was purchased by Burnaby, one of the city staff was going downstairs when she saw something before her. The young woman was shaken and would not talk about the incident, but from then on she refused to enter the building. The paranormal activity associated with Mathers House has diminished lately, but the feeling that the building is the home of an unsettling presence continues to make Burnaby employees uncomfortable.

FAIRACRES

"If the walls of Fairacres could talk, they would weep," Vancouver *Sun* reporter John Armstrong concluded in 1987.[3] Indeed, the history of the huge, three-storey mansion overlooking the lake is one of pain and sadness. There were a few good years, of course, but the 90-year-old structure seems to have retained within its walls considerably more sorrow than happiness. The ghosts who haunt this building, which was formerly the Burnaby Art Gallery and is now The Gallery at Ceperley House, are lugubrious creatures, aptly fitting the old home's sad past.

When Fairacres was completed, Vancouver was enjoying an economic boom. Writers boldly predicted that an industrial Vancouver would become the "Pittsburgh of the Pacific," while businessmen saw no end to the city's rapid growth. A wealthy and powerful business class was emerging; one member of this group was a Vancouver insurance and real estate tycoon, Henry Ceperley. Ceperley was born in New York State in 1851 and moved to British Columbia in 1886.

In 1909, Ceperley retired and, with his second wife, Grace, decided to build a country mansion in what was then rural Burnaby. Although not many miles from Vancouver, the Tudor-style mansion seemed remote. The dwelling overlooked the small lake, which was home to waterfowl and fish. "He is a most genial and companionable gentleman," wrote a biographer in 1914, "and has gained a host of warm friends during his residence in the northwest."[4] Ceperley seemed to enjoy the role of country squire, entertaining Vancouver society with extravagant parties at the mansion. Mrs. Ceperley preferred a quieter life. She was a very kind, caring person who spent many hours feeding the birds and tending her beautiful garden (which was overseen by an Asian gardener).

The Ceperleys lived at Fairacres for less than ten years. In 1917 Grace died, and when her will was probated it was discovered that she had owned the house and property. Under the terms of her will, the mansion would remain the home of her husband, but when he died, the money realized by the sale of the house was to be used to provide a children's playground at Stanley Park. Ceperley, faced with maintaining the home, first leased it, and then, ignoring the provisions of his wife's will, sold it in 1923. The Stanley Park playground received only $15,000.

The new owner of Fairacres was Frederick Buscombe who held the property for only a few years before it was sold to a family named Bogardus. The large home must have been very expensive to maintain as a private residence, even for Vancouver's wealthiest citizens, and eventually it was turned into an annex for the Vancouver General Hospital's tuberculosis ward. In the years before the introduction of anti-tubercular drugs, the mansion-cum-hospital was a place of considerable misery. After the annex was closed, Fairacres was briefly reconverted into a private residence and became home to Mr. and Mrs. Alexander Munro.

In 1939, the house was sold to the Benedictine order from Oregon. (The total price, incidentally, for the mansion and property was only $13,000.) Despite the order's strict discipline, and the fact that the now-middle-aged dwelling was inadequately heated, many of those who were at Westminster Priory (as it was called) during the 1940s and early 1950s have fond memories of their time there. In 1954, however, the order moved to a new abbey a few miles from Mission, and the Burnaby property was resold.

The next owner was the previously mentioned religious sect calling itself the Canadian Temple of the More Abundant Life, which also bought Mathers House. There were disturbing rumours about the practices in the live-in church school. The archbishop's ideas on education could be described as bizarre. The male teachers were required to grow beards, as their leader believed that facial hair acts as an "antenna," allowing the educator to pick up on the vibrations emitted by the universe.

There was a darker side to the school. The archbishop had a vicious temper, which was frequently unleashed on the children. On one occasion, when a six-year-old boy with a slight speech impediment couldn't keep up with the other children during the recital of the Lord's Prayer, Wolsey was enraged, and the boy was so traumatized by the incident that he reverted to baby talk.

In the face of a government probe into his educational methods, the archbishop closed the school in 1960. Four years later his church collapsed and Wolsey fled to the United States. While the whole truth of what happened at the school will never be known, those who have investigated the Fairacres hauntings conclude that many occurrences concern children.

After the collapse of the temple, Fairacres took on a new role: that of a university dormitory. In an era when "doing your own thing" meant rejecting tradition and everything the past stood for, the interior of the mansion was subjected to considerable defacement by the students. In 1966 the municipality of Burnaby purchased the building, but attempts by the local council to oust the students met with resistance. Shouting Marxist slogans they erected barricades, waved banners and even set fire to the beautiful hardwood floor in the billiard room. While the students eventually lost the battle, the greatest casualty was the once-magnificent mansion.

In 1967, Fairacres was reopened as Burnaby's project in honour of the Canadian Centennial: a new art gallery to serve the citizens of the municipality. At last the old mansion had regained some of the dignity it had lost in recent years, but the damage was not all physical. Fairacres was now haunted by the pain and suffering of its past; the gallery, it seems, has its complement of ghosts.

The first indication of strange occurrences came about the time the gallery first opened, when a night watchman reported seeing the spectre of Grace Ceperley upstairs. She was wearing a long, old-fashioned, flowing white dress, but even in the dim light he could tell her dress was transparent. The third floor, it should be noted, was originally designated as the children's rooms and Mrs. Ceperley was very fond of children.

There were also rumours during the early years of the gallery that other staff members have seen what many feel is the ghost of Mrs. Ceperley. The wispy outline of a woman in either a grey or blue evening dress has been reported walking along the open gallery area. One female staff member, it was said, even tried to talk to the apparition, but later refused to discuss the incident. As might be expected, many of the art gallery's employees have been reluctant to talk about such episodes.

To their credit some staff have freely described their experiences in the building. Maria Guerrero had been working in an office on the second floor for some time before she learned that the third floor was unused. Above her head, she frequently heard footsteps crossing the creaking wooden floors and going up the staircases, and a scraping noise such as that made by furniture being moved along the floor. "I didn't worry because I thought someone lived up there," she said. "The noises were so real."[5]

Early one evening in 1984, the program officer, Carol Defina, waited alone at the gallery's reception desk for other staff to arrive for a meeting. Suddenly, behind her, she heard a rustling sound,

The Gallery at Ceperley House (COURTESY OF D. M. BELYK)

like the swishing of a taffeta or satin dress or maybe even a crinoline. The sound was quite distinctive. As she later recalled:

> I was intent on preparing my notes and I heard a noise. I wasn't frightened, I looked over [to where the noise was coming from] and there was nothing there. About four minutes later the sound grew louder. My intuition warned me that something was trying to communicate. I knew that there was something there that was not of this world.[6]

Ms. Defina took her keys and waited for the others in her car. From then on she refused to work alone during the evening at the gallery.

Many staff members believe that a second ghost, a man seen standing at the top of the staircase, also haunts the old building. There have been other strange occurrences as well. Mark Stevens was working on the main floor one evening in 1984, preparing the walls for an exhibition, while another staff member, Robert Lagasse, was working in the basement. Because it was after closing, the building's alarm system was turned on. As he worked, Stevens became aware of the noise of someone walking diagonally from a bedroom balcony across to the opposite end of the second floor. Because there was no carpeting on the floor at the time, the sound was quite distinctive: someone in stocking feet or maybe soft slippers was pressing down on the old floor.

Stevens phoned his colleague, Lagasse, in the basement. Together the two men searched the building thoroughly but to their surprise, no one was hiding there. As far as Stevens was concerned it was impossible. "If [the intruder] went out the French doors the alarm would have gone off. There were no open windows, and even if there were, it's a long two-storey drop, 25 feet or more."[7]

A year earlier, Lagasse had had his own unnerving experience while working late in the basement removing prints from their frames. The job required the use of a hammer and a screwdriver. When he had separated a large number of prints and frames he moved the art work to the floor, out of his way. When he turned around again he found his hammer and screwdriver weren't on the bench where he had left them, but were hanging up in their proper place on the tool rack. To Lagasse the incident did not seem particularly unusual. He thought that he might have absent-mindedly replaced the tools in the rack. He removed the hammer and screwdriver from the rack and continued to work on the prints and frames.

After a few minutes he picked up the separated frames and took them to the storage room to be put away. While he reached into his pocket for his keys, he noticed that the padlock on the door was swinging to and fro on its own. The lock continued its motion for as long as Lagasse watched, which was several minutes. When he returned to his workbench his tools were again not where he had left them. They had been returned to their place on the rack. "Then I got this cold feeling on the back of my neck ... I knew something was different, the atmosphere had changed."[8]

By late 1985, the Vancouver press was beginning to take an interest in the ghosts at the gallery. In December of that year,

Vancouver *Province* assistant city editor, Damian Inwood, and a photographer, Les Brazso, arranged to spend the night in the reputedly haunted gallery. After an unremarkable evening, the two made themselves as comfortable as possible in the billiard room. Before climbing into their sleeping bags, they set up a small voice-activated tape recorder, just in case.

Some time in the night the journalist awoke abruptly. "I felt that something had nudged my subconscious, trying to attract my attention, and I was suddenly afraid," he wrote later. "A chilling presence seemed to be pushing its way into the room and filling it."[9]

Inwood tried to scream, but nothing happened; he tried to move but found he couldn't bring his body to a sitting position. He looked across at his companion but he was fast asleep in his sleeping bag. Then suddenly the terrible weight of the presence seemed to lift. The icy chill left the air and everything was back to normal.

Inwood remained awake the remainder of the night. In the morning he checked his recorder. "I expected to hear myself crying out in my sleep. Instead, sandwiched between our conversations, was a weird warble followed by a hissing silence." Whether it was an ordinary nightmare or something more, the incident was very unsettling. The journalist made no plans to spend another night in the gallery. Two years later a Vancouver *Sun* reporter, John Armstrong, repeated the experiment. For Armstrong, however, the night was uneventful.

An obvious question concerns the identity of the ghosts who haunt the gallery and one candidate is Grace Ceperley. That the provisions of her will were not carried out may be the reason for this restless spirit. Ghosts elsewhere have needed even less excuse to do their haunting. There are apparently many other ghosts who haunt Fairacres though strangely, as far as is known, there were no tragic deaths of the kind that seem to leave a psychic "impression" on a structure for years after the event.

There may be one clue to the other presences. Early in 1987, a well-known psychic, Joan Fontaine, visited Fairacres with a television crew. Ms. Fontaine's "reading" of the gallery was later broadcast on the CBC, and as might be expected, the psychic pronounced the gallery a very troubled place. She could sense children pleading for help, but she said more, not all of which was broadcast on the program. As part of his final report, the departing gallery director, Roger Boulet, wrote that Ms. Fontaine had expressed her impression that much of the unhappiness associated with the house concerned the abuse of children. "These episodes," he concluded, "seem to relate to the occupancy of the building by the Society of the Foundation for a More Abundant Life."[10]

During her first two years as gallery director, Lina Jabra stated that she had experienced no strange incidents. By 1990, it was hoped that the wonderful light of the beautiful artwork hanging on exhibit in the gallery would overcome the darkness of Fairacres' past. This, however, would not be the case.

More on Ceperley House

In 1990, visitor Margaret Hambrook was attending a party at the gallery. When she went upstairs to see the large master bedroom on the second floor, Mrs. Hambrook suddenly felt a hand grab her ankle as she passed the threshold. Fortunately, she was able to take hold of the door frame, which prevented her from sprawling to the floor. The force of the hand was unmistakable; it prevented the forward movement of her leg. She believed that "someone was not pleased that I was in the house."[11]

During the winter of 1997, a woman — a frequent visitor to the gallery — arrived to visit an exhibition sponsored by the gallery. Her dog was usually with her, and because the pet was so well behaved he was permitted to accompany her on her visits. On this day, though, he refused to set foot inside the gallery and had to be taken back to her car.

The woman examined the collection on the main floor and then proceeded up the stairway to the second floor. After viewing this exhibit she went into the art-rental gallery to look at the works available for lease. Engrossed as she was in her study of the art she failed to pay attention to her reflection in the window that dominated one wall of the room.

Finally, she happened to glance toward the window and was shocked, for the image wasn't her own. Instead, she saw a woman with hands folded, wearing a long, old-fashioned white dress. The visitor was dressed in contemporary clothes including a ski jacket (which was more appropriate to the year and the season). She quickly descended the stairs and told the gallery staff what she had seen. The staff checked the room, but nothing out of the ordinary was found. When the visitor attempted to bring her dog into the gallery so that he could have a look, he again refused to enter.

Although the ghost or ghosts have apparently not been seen since, the house remains an eerie place at night and staff members admit they do not like to remain there alone after the sun goes down. It is interesting to note that even staff members who claim not to believe in ghosts are struck by the creepy ambience that is so closely associated with the gallery.

Until 1999, the facility had been operated by a non-profit board, but in that year it was taken over by the city and operated as the Gallery at Ceperley House. It is currently being restored so that it will reflect the splendour achieved briefly by Henry and Grace Ceperley. Because of the changes to the structure instituted by the Canadian Temple of the More Abundant Life and the damage to the third floor by the university students, the task is indeed difficult.

* * * * *

Incidentally, Fairacres is not the first-known haunted art gallery in British Columbia. During the 1950s, Theo Hare operated Victoria's Norfolk Gallery on Broad Street. Hare was a popular figure in Victoria art circles and his sudden death one day while working in his gallery was a shock to all those who knew him.

In due course Katie Bloomfield reopened the gallery under a new name. Soon afterwards, Mrs. Bloomfield discovered that the former owner had not exactly vacated the premises. As she recalled:

> I saw him one night ... I had to go down the corridor past [Mr. Hare's old office] and he appeared in the doorway. I couldn't go into the kitchen some nights because I felt someone was there. The hair stood up on my neck.[12]

According to Mrs. Bloomfield the spectre wasn't solid but was the "shape of a man" leaning on the frame of the door. She added ominously that she felt there was "something else" upstairs, and she wouldn't go there at night or even in the daytime if she was alone.

A few years later, the gallery was taken over and operated by Chris Phillips and his wife, Alma. Like Mrs. Bloomfield, they soon discovered that there were strange goings-on at the gallery. Both Mr. and Mrs. Phillips claimed to have seen the misty figure of a man in the corridor by Mr. Hare's office. The couple was not the only witnesses: one day their four-year-old son reported that a strange man had come into his room at night and sat on his bed. The living quarters the Phillips family occupied were secure, and there was no way that the boy's visitor could have been a living human being. While his parents were much disturbed by the occurrence, the little boy thought nothing of it.

The Phillips family closed the gallery in 1960 and moved away from Victoria. As far as is known, there were no further reports of the spectral presence at the Broad Street address.

Stately Old Haunts

As some of British Columbia's stately old houses are bought up by the government for use as museums, art galleries and the like, the presences of private homes become the ghosts of public institutions. Many of the people involved in the operation of museums or galleries are not keen on mentioning their resident ghosts, but they are there, nonetheless.

TOD HOUSE: THE GHOST WHO HATED CHRISTMAS

The pleasant-looking white bungalow today seems quite ordinary, though it doubtless has lost some of the charm it once had. Years ago it stood far back from the road in a beautiful orchard which extended all the way down to the sea. It is easy to imagine what it would have been like living there in the spring, amid the glory of the pink blossoms.

Of course, times change. Now the trees are all gone. Instead, the dwelling stands in the middle of a comfortable block on a quiet street in the Victoria suburb of Oak Bay, and the only hint that the house might be older than its neighbours is that it is built diagonally on the property. This means it takes up more than a normal-size lot; no modern builder would waste so much valuable land. Indeed, by British Columbia standards the house is ancient — well over

150 years old. But that's not all that makes it interesting. At least one ghost haunts the dark recesses of Tod House.

* * * * *

When they purchased Tod House in late 1944, retired Colonel and Mrs. T. C. Evans were highly sceptical of the ghost stories their neighbours told them. According to Oak Bay locals, Tod House was definitely haunted and they would have been well advised never to have moved in. However, as a former military man with a very practical view of the world, Colonel Evans simply didn't believe in ghosts. Mrs. Evans was also unimpressed by such stories, so the neighbourhood gossip was all but ignored.

Not long after the colonel and Mrs. Evans moved into their new home they began to change their minds; the Tod House ghost intended to make its presence felt. What emerged during the next seven years was one of the best-documented hauntings in Canadian history.

Colonel and Mrs. Evans hardly had time to unpack their belongings before they were faced with a number of occurrences that defied logical explanation. Objects that were suspended on hooks in the kitchen began rocking on their own. The door leading from the kitchen to a particularly dark and uninviting cellar would not stay shut, even after it was carefully latched. Filing down the slot that held the latch should have solved the problem but it didn't; neither did jamming a chair against the door at night. Often the next morning the chair would be found several feet away from where it had been placed, while the cellar door would be standing ajar again. (Finally, in order to keep it shut, it was necessary to put an additional bolt on the door.)

Although shaking up the new owners quite badly at first, the presence did not seem really malevolent. The ghost had very definite likes and dislikes. It appeared to be particularly fond of Mrs. Evans's antique rocker. Frequently the rocker, which had been placed in the living room, would be seen to rock on its own. While the ghost seemed to enjoy this activity, the couple did not. They found the rocking very unnerving. Only when the chair was moved into the hall did the rocking finally stop.

The ghost, on the other hand, had a strong dislike of all kinds of hats. Several times the couple would discover that hats which had been placed neatly on the hat rack by the front door had been taken down and scattered like leaves after an autumn storm, all over the hall floor. They would patiently pick up all the hats only to face the same situation again some time later.

Strangely, although it was downstairs where most of the ghostly activity took place, it was in one of the upstairs rooms that the visitation was most strongly felt. The Evanses had decided to use a large upstairs room as the master bedroom, but after spending only a couple of nights there, they moved to another bedroom. Neither the colonel nor Mrs. Evans was able to put their finger on what the feeling was like exactly, but there was undoubtedly something strange about that room, and they avoided spending another night there. As they discovered years later, their fears about that room were well-founded.

One night there was a tremendous crash from an area of grass at the side of the house. When the colonel rushed out to investigate, he found one of the large bedroom windows, still in its frame, lying on the lawn. It had come from what was known as the "eerie room." When Colonel Evans examined the frame he found that it was in excellent condition, with the nails still in place. It looked as though someone possessing superhuman strength had pushed the window out by its frame, and sent it crashing to the grass below.

The unusual occurrences that were taking place now almost regularly had piqued Colonel and Mrs. Evans's curiosity. They had no idea who (or, indeed, what) was perpetrating these phenomena or why it haunted this particular house. Newspaper stories about John Tod, the first owner, were often full of errors. Only later did an accurate picture of the fur trader emerge.

Tod was born in Dumbartonshire, Scotland, in 1794, and attended the local parish school until he was 16 years old. In 1811 he came to North America to work for the Hudson's Bay Company. He was a complex character. He was clever, but he certainly had a grudge against authority, which frequently led him into difficulties with his employers. Hudson's Bay Company Governor

Tod House. (THE HERITAGE GROUP COLLECTION)

George Simpson regarded him as a bully whose manners were uncouth and banished him to isolated New Caledonia (an area which includes much of present-day British Columbia) where the fur trader would spend most of his career. Tod had four long-term relationships during his life and was formally married twice. He had children by all four women.

In 1850, Tod retired from the Hudson's Bay Company, and soon began construction of a house on his 109-acre Oak Bay farm. After spending more than 20 years together, Tod and his common-law wife, Sophia Lolo, were married in 1863. Tod's relationship with Sophia appears to have remained close until his death in 1882.

The retired trader did not impress all of Victoria's residents. In an age of conformity, Tod was a nonconformist. He had given up the Presbyterian faith of his parents and looked with disfavour on all organized religions. In his later years, he became interested in spiritualism and attended a number of seances. Among the conservative residents of rural Oak Bay, such notions were regarded as bizarre.

John Tod lived to be a very old man and, when he finally died, the house passed to his heirs. There is no record that either Tod or his descendants were haunted by what came to be known as the Tod House ghost but then, Tod's family could have had good reason to keep the story of the family ghost to themselves. The old trader may have almost literally had a skeleton in his closet.

Meanwhile, Colonel and Mrs. Evans continued to experience the presence. During the first Christmas they occupied the house, the couple spent many hours decorating; on Christmas Eve they were both very tired so they retired to bed early. They apparently slept soundly and heard nothing during the night. When they awoke on Christmas morning they were astonished to discover that all the decorations had been pulled down from the walls and off the tree and were piled neatly in the middle of the living-room floor. The presence, they felt, was trying to tell them something. The colonel added another line to the emerging profile of the Tod House ghost. "The ghost," he wrote, "also hated Christmas."[1]

While the Evanses never saw the ghost themselves, there was one terrifying incident the year after they had taken possession of Tod House. As was their habit during the Second World War, Colonel and Mrs. Evans invited two airmen into their home to spend weekend leave.

Since neither man seemed to be the squeamish type, Mrs. Evans elected to put them in the one bedroom that received little use — the one that the couple had used briefly as a master bedroom a year earlier. The room had been completely refurbished with new wallpaper and fresh paint, and it must have seemed absurd not to use it for guests.

When Mrs. Evans arose the next day, she was surprised to find the guest room empty. It appeared to have been vacated suddenly: the blankets and sheets lay in a twisted mess on the bed. It was only long after the morning sun had risen that the guests returned. According to them, the night had begun normally enough, but before it ended both were frightened almost out of their wits. The account of one of the servicemen was later recorded in a newspaper:

> We had been asleep for several hours when I suddenly awoke. I can't really describe what woke me, although it sounded like the rattling of chains. Over in the corner stood an Indian woman, her hands held out toward me in such a manner that she seemed to be pleading with me to help her.
> On her arms and legs were what looked like fetters. She kept looking at me, her hands outstretched and saying something that I couldn't catch. As suddenly as she appeared she was gone. I'll never forget the sight.[2]

The story of the chained Indian woman was particularly interesting to the colonel. During his research into the history of Tod House he had learned that it was rumoured that one of Tod's Indian wives had gone mad and was kept chained in an upstairs bedroom. The story related by the unfortunate guest (the second man apparently woke up only after the figure had disappeared) lent validity to this tale, since the man had no notion of the history of Tod House.

While the ghost had caused them considerable anguish when they first moved into the old house, the couple gradually became accustomed to its presence. If not exactly part of the family, it seemed like an (usually) unobtrusive lodger padding silently about the house. At times having the ghost about was even pleasant. "There's one thing about it," Mrs. Evans observed. "You're never lonely with these invisible personages around. I don't ever feel I am alone."[3]

However, for those unaccustomed to the ghost, an encounter with it could be frightening. The Evanses had lived in the house several years when they decided to hold a New Year's Eve party. The evening was well under way when suddenly a guest noticed something strange. In the kitchen there was a massive stone fireplace, part of the original house. Set in the stonework was a hook upon which Mrs. Evans had hung a porcelain biscuit jar. As the guests watched almost mesmerized, the jar swung to and fro on the hook. The movement continued unabated for about 35 minutes before finally stopping. Despite Colonel Evans's attempt to reassure everyone that it was really quite a routine event at Tod House, the moving biscuit jar severely upset a number of guests that night.

The Tod House ghost, which had been the subject of neighbourhood gossip for many years, suddenly became a matter of broader public interest. Victoria and Vancouver newspapers picked up the story, while reporters trekked out to Oak Bay to interview the Evanses. Some journalists were even fortunate enough to witness strange events themselves, including the mysterious moving cookie jar and the cellar door that opened by itself. Other reporters succeeded in tracking down the previous owner of the house, Mrs. E. C. Turner. Mrs. Turner who, with her daughter, had occupied Tod House from 1929 until she sold it in 1944, was no less familiar with the ghost than Colonel and Mrs. Evans.

"Sometimes I would awake at night feeling a presence in my room," reported Mrs. Turner. "The door would slowly open although I couldn't see anything. I am still fully convinced that there was someone there." If Mrs. Turner couldn't see anything, there was one member of her household that apparently could — her cat. And what that little animal saw must have been scary indeed. "At night the cat would suddenly growl and arch her back and her fur would stand up," Mrs. Turner recalled. "I feel sure that she saw something that I could not see."[4]

What was interesting, also, was that Mrs. Turner shared Colonel and Mrs. Evans's feelings regarding the "eerie room." Neither the woman nor her daughter would spend the night in that room. However, unlike the Evanses, who grew accustomed to the ghost, Mrs. Turner found that it wore her down. "Sometimes as I walked along the passageway, I felt that someone was walking behind me. It got very tiresome," she confessed.

Suddenly psychic experts offered all sorts of explanations and advice. Wrote one medium: "It is an indication that in the past someone was terribly unhappy in the house and has returned now to try and find the happiness they missed."[5]

However, no one was quite sure how to exorcise the unhappy ghost from the premises. One expert advised leaving a pad and pencil in plain view, so the ghost could communicate. Another suggested leaving out a pail of water, because sometimes that placated a restless soul from the "other world." In this case, neither approach was successful. Doors continued to open, hats flew and jars, alas, rocked.

Canada's fascination with the Tod House ghost reached its peak early in 1947, when the story was aired on the CBC. By then the owners were subjected to a continual stream of cars driving slowly by to get a look at the haunted house. Colonel and Mrs. Evans would be startled to see little children with their faces pushed up against the glass of the downstairs windows, looking for the ghost. After the broadcast, the couple was inundated with mail. While many of the letters were from cranks, a number of people wrote to express their sympathy. One measure of the popularity of the ghost house was a letter the colonel received from Oakville, Ontario. The address read simply, "Colonel Evans, the Haunted House, Victoria." It found its way to the house without difficulty.

For a retired couple like the Evanses, the publicity associated with the haunted house was most unwelcome, and they were relieved when public interest began to fade. In 1947, the colonel undertook much-needed renovations to the dwelling and among the planned improvements was the installation of an oil-burning furnace to replace the old wood-and-coal burner. Colonel Evans hired two men to do the difficult labour, digging a very deep hole beside the front porch to accommodate the oil-storage tank. When they had reached a depth of seven feet, the shovel of one of the men struck something unexpected. It was a soft, porous material that crumbled easily in the hand. The colonel studied it closely. Despite its terribly deteriorated condition, there was no mistaking what it was — pieces of a human skeleton.

The colonel asked the workmen to uncover all the bones, but the men refused. Even after he offered them a substantial bonus to finish the job, the men continued to demand more. They were, of course, aware that Tod House already had a frightening reputation and, in the end, the colonel had to do the job himself.

What he found in the ground by his house was a human skeleton, complete except, curiously, for the head. Colonel Evans had the bones examined by an anatomist. The remains, it was reported, were those of an Oriental or a Native Indian woman. Because of their poor condition, it was difficult to estimate how long the bones had been buried, but certainly more than 50 years. Similarly, the cause of death could not be determined. As to why the bones were so badly decomposed, it was the opinion of the anatomist that the woman's body had been buried in quick-lime.

Some people maintained that the bones showed that old John Tod had been involved in smuggling Orientals into the area, but there was not a shred of evidence to support this thesis. It seemed more likely that the unfortunate woman was someone close to John Tod: someone, if the rumours were correct, who had known long years of torment and madness.

There is one more intriguing twist to this story. Once the bones were removed from the unmarked grave, the haunting of Tod House abruptly ceased. Although a number of mediums continued to predict the return of the spirit to John Tod's old farmhouse, it never came back to haunt Colonel and Mrs. Evans. Yet the loss of their visitor must have been a mixed blessing. As the Evanses admitted, they had grown used to the presence of their ghost.

There is a brief footnote to the Tod House haunting. In 1971, after the colonel's death, the property changed hands again. For the new owner, the value of Tod House as a historical site had to be weighed against the cost of maintaining such an old building. Also, at a time of rapidly escalating real estate prices, the large piece of property on which the house stood was very valuable.

On June 24, 1974, the house was again in the news when the Oak Bay Municipal Council moved to declare Tod House a heritage landmark, which meant that no major changes could be made to the structure without the approval of council. Some time later the house was purchased by the municipality of Oak Bay and the provincial government. Currently, it is administered by a board appointed jointly by the two levels of government.

Has the ghost returned to Tod House as many seers have predicted? According to some, the spirit has never entirely left its haunt. Some people have reported seeing the latch on the door to the cellar lift on its own and the door swing open. This is followed by a blast of cold air that sweeps up the stairs and into the kitchen. Even with such disturbances, though, the ghostly activity at Victoria's oldest house remains relatively subdued. At least the Christmas decorations remain where they are.

IRVING HOUSE

One historic British Columbia residence claiming a ghost or two is New Westminster's Irving House. Begun in 1862 by the Royal Engineers, the handsome, 14-room home stands on the side of a hill overlooking the Fraser River. The first owner of the house was William Irving, a Scottish riverboat captain who immigrated to British Columbia via Oregon in 1859. Captain Irving established his family in Victoria, initially, and began a ferry service between the Fraser River goldfields and the coast. The Irving family occupied their new house on the mainland in 1864. Captain Irving, however, did not have many years to enjoy his home; eight years later, at the age of 56, he succumbed to pneumonia.

The house remained in the possession of Captain Irving's descendants until 1950, when it was sold to the city of New Westminster as a historic site. Today Irving House has been painstakingly restored to represent the period between 1864 and 1890. Fortunately, in 1950, city fathers had the good sense to purchase the furnishings, and many of the items in the house are Irving originals. Irving House is now part of New Westminster's museum complex on Royal Avenue.

The museum's curator, Archie Miller, has had a few strange experiences in the old house. He has occupied an apartment in the dwelling since 1973, and over the years has become familiar with every creak and groan the old house makes but, as he states, there are some occurrences that cannot be readily explained.

Early one morning in 1980, Miller was awakened by the low growling of his Norwegian elkhound, Sapper, who was beside his bed. The dog was very agitated. Miller could see his fur bristling. "I knew something wasn't right."[6]

At first the curator assumed that there was an intruder on the property — someone walking on the porch — but as he listened, he realized the sound wasn't outside the house; it was inside. Above his head he could hear footsteps in the upstairs hall. The noise was quite distinctive, Miller recalled — like the sound of a full-grown man pacing the hall. Miller and his dog proceeded up the staircase. He ordered Sapper to guard the bottom of the stairs while he checked the outside of the house. He could find no evidence of a break-in. He returned to the bottom of the stairs, but by then the footsteps had stopped. He went upstairs and again there was no sign of a break-in.

As Miller thought about the incident later, he continued to be puzzled. "It made no sense that someone would be walking back and forth above me. After all, it would have been strange behaviour for a thief, pacing like that." Moreover, even if the intruder had succeeded in sneaking in earlier, there was no way he could manage to escape from the locked house.

"I've had people tell me it's only the house creaking, but I've lived here over 15 years and I've come to know the sounds that belong and the sounds that don't belong. And these sounds definitely didn't belong."

There was another incident about a year later. Miller and two tour guides were just closing up after the last visitor had left, when suddenly one of the women called out that she heard something upstairs. His first thought, of course, was that one of the visitors had stayed back and hidden somewhere. As the guides waited below, Miller went up the main staircase.

Suddenly he was aware that something was happening. "As I approached the top two or three stairs, I had the feeling someone was coming down." Instinctively he flattened himself against the wall to let whomever it was pass by. Quite shaken, he called down to the guides at the bottom of the steps, asking if they saw anything. "No," they said, peering up at the curator who was still pressed against the wall. "But what are you doing?" As in the previous incident, Miller's search of the house revealed no intruder or sign of a break-in.

Miller has not seen anything unusual in Irving House, but some visitors have, on a number of occasions. Some time ago, there were two different reports of similar ghostly sightings — a small woman wearing an old-fashioned, dark-coloured dress — in the house. Interestingly, at the time of the incidents, both witnesses reported hearing the rustle of clothes. The museum staff found these occurrences interesting because they came from two people unfamiliar with the history of the Irving House ghost, yet their descriptions of the spectre were almost identical.

There have been other reports. Some time ago, before Miller became curator, a little girl, about four years old, rushed up to

Irving House. (COURTESY OF NEW WESTMINSTER PUBLIC LIBRARY)

her mother while they were touring the restored house and, pointing to one of the cordoned-off bedrooms, said, "If I'm not allowed to go in there, why is that man allowed to lie on the bed?" The child's mother saw no one, but she noted that the bed had been mussed up in a manner that suggested a full-grown person had been lying on it. As staff members observed, there was certainly no adult in the house who was likely to lie on one of the carefully arranged exhibits.

Unlike presences in other houses, the Irving House ghosts are the gentle kind. Indeed, the Irvings were a close family, and the house, over the years, knew more joy than sorrow. Who are the ghosts of Irving House? Many believe that the female spectre is either Elizabeth Irving, Captain Irving's wife, or their daughter, Mary. Both women spent many years in the house and were very attached to it. Mrs. Irving continued to live in the house for 13 years after the death of the captain; however, in 1885 she moved to Portland, Oregon, where she remarried. It was said this second marriage ended badly, and it is possible she longed for the happier days in her New Westminster home. She died in Portland in 1922.

The Irvings' eldest daughter, Mary, married Thomas Briggs in 1874. Prior to Mrs. Irving's move to Portland, Thomas Briggs purchased the Irving family home from his mother-in-law and he and his wife raised nine children there. Mary Briggs remained in the house until her death in 1931.

There is still the question of the heavy footsteps upstairs. Some believe they are the footsteps of a man crushed by a wagonload of wood on the street near the house in 1871. The badly injured man was carried into Irving House where he died a short time later. A more likely candidate for the footsteps, however, is Captain Irving himself. The captain was a man of tremendous drive, who would not have left this earth willingly, and there is more evidence: apparently he had the habit of pacing. On his ships, others noted that he frequently paced the entire length of the quarterdeck. It is possible that it was the captain's ghost that Miller and his dog, Sapper, heard so distinctly that night.

There was one occasion involving a rather unpleasant spectre when Miller was away from the house on a trip. A friend of his, a big burly fellow who was not afraid of anything, offered to house-sit while the curator was gone. All went well until one evening when the man believed he heard a creaking noise in the house. Unsure of what was going on, he began to search. When he came into the front hall, he met something entirely unexpected: the figure of a man standing on the front porch, looking through the glass of the door. The man was plainly visible and as Miller's friend later reported, he did not look happy at all. The house-sitter was so shaken by the figure he ran to St. Mary's Hospital next door to Irving House, and it was some time before he regained his composure and returned to the old dwelling.

Captain William Irving. (COURTESY OF NEW
WESTMINSTER PUBLIC LIBRARY)

Some would argue that there was nothing supernatural about the incident at all, that Miller's friend had simply seen a prowler looking in the front-door window. However, according to Miller, there's one problem with that explanation: the glass in the door is opaque, and it is normally quite impossible to tell who is standing on the front porch.

POINT ELLICE HOUSE

"I stood in the drawing room of the old house, home to three generations of the O'Reilly family, trying to come to a decision. I had an uncanny feeling I was not alone."[7]

The year was 1965, and the decision facing Inez O'Reilly and her husband, John, was crucial to the continued existence of Point Ellice House. As heir to the century-old dwelling which had originally been built by his grandfather, Peter O'Reilly, John had received a generous offer for the property. If he and his wife accepted, it would mean Point Ellice House would fall to the wrecker's ball. While the couple would feel the loss of the house as a severe blow, maintaining a dwelling so old was also a great responsibility. If they decided to keep Point Ellice House, the dilapidated old structure would have to undergo considerable restoration.

In the end, the couple made what they felt was the only right decision — somehow they would find the money for repairs. Point Ellice House would be saved for a little while longer. It would be a tragedy to lose this wonderful piece of Victoria history, and also, Mrs. O'Reilly felt that she and John were not the only residents of Point Ellice House. The ghosts who occupied the one-storey, 15-room structure were not disposed to losing their home either.

Point Ellice House, with Irving House, shares the distinction of being one of the oldest houses in the province. Built between 1865 and 1867, the dwelling was in its day one of the finest homes in Victoria. O'Reilly, a native of County Meath, Ireland, came to British Columbia in 1859. Because of his experience in the Irish

Point Ellice House. (THE HERITAGE GROUP COLLECTION)

Revenue Police, young O'Reilly was made the stipendiary magistrate for the community of Fort Langley and within two years, Governor James Douglas had appointed him magistrate and gold commissioner for the all-important Cariboo district.

While O'Reilly spent much of his time in the interior of British Columbia, he chose to have his house built in the civilized city of Victoria. Peter and his wife Caroline — he had married the sister of British Columbia's first lieutenant-governor, Sir Joseph Trutch — built their home on the banks of the narrow inlet known as the Gorge. There the O'Reillys raised their family, two boys and a girl. In the 1880s and 90s the house was the scene of elaborate parties and other social events attended by the cream of Victoria society.

Kathleen O'Reilly, daughter of Peter and Caroline, never married, remaining at Point Ellice House until her death in 1945. It is not surprising, then, that there are those who feel Miss O'Reilly remains even now within its walls.

As the years passed the O'Reilly family faced a considerable problem: the house was in the wrong place. While the location had once been singularly attractive, overlooking as it did the Selkirk Water of Victoria's Inner Harbour, the other fine residences which had shared the locale were sold and pulled down to make way for industry. By the mid-1960s, Point Ellice House was among the last of the grand old homes that had been built there.

In 1967, after spending two years rebuilding the house, John and Inez O'Reilly opened Point Ellice House as a private museum. As at Irving House, some visitors saw more than the curators intended. Soon after the house was opened to the public, Mrs. O'Reilly received a complaint from one woman visitor regarding the ghosts which had frightened her small granddaughter. "You should warn people that the house is haunted," the angry woman demanded. "We should sue you. It's very dangerous."[8]

There were other instances, however, where the ghosts were helpful; in one case, a mysterious woman in an old-fashioned blue dress showed a visiting family around the house. There was no one in the house at the time that fit the family's description, but the dress was real enough — their description matched one that was once worn by Kathleen O'Reilly. Another time, two male visitors claimed that they had seen the apparition of a woman who fit Kathleen's description waiting for them as they arrived. When the young men left, they said the figure followed them down the road.

The ghost of Miss O'Reilly does not seem to be alone. In 1971, a well-known American psychic, Suzie Smith, paid a visit, and she could sense not just one presence, but as many as four. They were there, it seems, to help keep the museum tidy, although Ms. Smith didn't explain how the ghosts accomplished this. One of the presences haunting the house is likely to be Caroline O'Reilly, the first mistress of Point Ellice House. The elder Mrs. O'Reilly was very attached to her home, so it would not be surprising that she has remained behind. However, the identities of the other presences are not clear.

In 1974, the house was sold to the provincial government and is now administered by the Heritage Branch. Since then, there have been no ghostly goings-on reported by museum staff members.

More on Point Ellice House

In the summer of 2000, Ann Wise was visiting Victoria with her husband. Knowing that he would be engaged elsewhere, she made plans to visit two interesting tourist destinations: Emily Carr House, which had been home to British Columbia's most famous artist, and Point Ellice House. She had never been to either of the residences before and knew little about the houses themselves. What was appealing about Point Ellice House was that the staff served "real" English tea in the afternoon so Ann decided to go there after her morning tour of Emily Carr House.

She had no idea that her venue for the following day included one supposedly haunted house. However, "That night I had a very vivid dream of a dining room full of guests, and a lady in a blue dress. The dress was high-collared and her hair was swept up on top of her head. Towards the end of the dream, I realized she was [partially transparent] and was a ghost."[9]

Ann wondered if her vivid dream had a connection with one of the historic houses she planned to visit. When she reached Emily Carr House she asked the staff if the old house was haunted, but no one working there thought so. Ann walked the few miles between the two historic sites and arrived at Point Ellice House in time to be served afternoon tea in the garden. As she recalled, "I told them about the dream, and one of the staff brought out some old photos of the [house's former] inhabitants, and it was then I realized the similarities between Ms. [Kathleen] O'Reilly and the lady from my dream. The hairstyle was the same, albeit the lady in the dream seemed a bit plumper than the photo. They told me that a blue dress of the kind I described was hanging in the closet." For Ann, the house seemed disturbingly familiar.

Later she and her husband visited Ross Bay Cemetery to view the grave of Emily Carr. "Naturally, we wandered around viewing the graves of other dignitaries. Coming close to one gravestone from the back, I got severe goosebumps all over ..." To her shock, when she walked around to view the monument from the front, she discovered it was for the O'Reilly family.

ROYAL ROADS

In the best tradition of other military academies, including West Point in the United States, Royal Roads Military College, not far from Victoria, had its own ghost. The Royal Roads ghost was seen many times by the cadets in residence there, but unfortunately none of these incidents were documented, and with the rapid turnover of students attending the school, the accounts have tended to be taken away with each graduating class. As far as can be determined, the Royal Roads haunting predates 1940, when the college was established. Before the building was purchased by the defence department, it had been the home of the James Dunsmuir family.

James Dunsmuir, the son of the Vancouver Island coal baron, Robert Dunsmuir, played an important role in the political life of this province; he served first as premier, then as lieutenant-governor, though politics, generally, were not to the taste of this very reserved man. When he resigned as premier on November 21, 1902, he had filled the position for less than three years. In 1906 he was appointed to the largely ceremonial office of lieutenant-governor. He retired from public life in 1909, and died in 1920.

During his time as lieutenant-governor, while the family lived at Government House, Dunsmuir decided to construct a residence befitting his exalted social station. Earlier, in 1892, three years after the death of his father, he had built a home for himself and his family on the banks of Victoria's Gorge. Burleith, as it was called, was an attractive mansion, but quite modest — at least in terms of Craigdarroch Castle, James's mother's palatial residence in Victoria.

The new Dunsmuir mansion was a huge, Norman-styled affair with 600 acres of formal gardens and treed parkland. Hatley Park, as the Dunsmuirs called their new home, was lavish in the extreme. "Money doesn't matter," James Dunsmuir was reported to have told the contractors. "Just build what I want." The result was arguably the most beautiful private residence in the province, surpassing even Craigdarroch.

The building was huge: there were a dozen bedrooms and nine bathrooms in the main wing alone. Extra features included a third-floor ballroom which could be reached by elevator. When it was finally completed in 1908, the Dunsmuirs' new home had cost an estimated $4,000,000 and the expenses didn't stop there: a staff of a hundred was needed just to maintain the mansion, the gardens and six miles of roads on the property. After the completion of Hatley Park, Laura Dunsmuir, James's wife, and her daughters gave many magnificent parties there. Attending such galas were not only the local celebrities, but also many important members of the British aristocracy. James Dunsmuir, however, was becoming more and more a recluse — he shunned these social events.

In 1929, nine years after the death of James Dunsmuir, the New York stock market crashed, and much of Laura Dunsmuir's wealth was wiped out virtually overnight. It is not difficult to imagine how Mrs. Dunsmuir, a member of what until recently had been British Columbia's most important family, suffered during this period. She had lost almost everything. She attempted to meet at least some of the cost of maintaining Hatley Park by opening the gardens to the public for a fee, but during the Depression, few people could afford the luxury of a garden visit. Stories began to circulate in Victoria that Laura Dunsmuir was almost destitute, that creditors held off foreclosing on the property only because the elderly woman was so ill.

Mrs. Dunsmuir passed away in 1937 and Hatley Park remained empty for almost four years. A small staff was retained to maintain the property. Soon after Mrs. Dunsmuir's death one of the maids reported that she felt uncomfortable there — as though someone unseen was watching her as she went about her work. The feeling was so intense that she was reluctant to go into some of the rooms alone.

In 1940 the estate was purchased by the defence department for $75,000 — less than the original cost of the stone fence which surrounds the property. The following year Hatley Park was turned into a school to train naval officers, who, because of the war, were in short supply. The fact that the building was now the property of the navy did nothing to lessen its increasingly eerie reputation.

A recent photo of Hatley Park, now a university. (THE HERITAGE GROUP)

Students working late at night claimed to be suddenly overcome by a strange feeling — like coming into contact with a mass of freezing cobwebs. This feeling usually occurred on the second and third floors of the building.

Although details are scarce, students have admitted seeing the apparition of a little old woman standing by their beds. A Royal Roads Public Information Officer, Captain Martin Marshall, recalled one incident when he was still a cadet at the institution.

A cadet who was acting as senior duty officer appeared one morning quite pale and shaken and told a most unusual tale. He had fallen asleep the previous night but some time in the early hours of the morning he was awakened by someone pulling his leg. As he opened his eyes he saw the apparition of a woman before him. He tried to shake his leg from her grip but the spectre held on. As strong as the young cadet was, it took considerable effort to break free, but once he did manage to loosen her hold, the spectre disappeared.

It is perhaps not surprising that the spirit of the mistress of Hatley Park would return to her home; during the last years of her life the fate of the family mansion was probably very much on her mind. Moreover, it is possible to imagine what she might think to see so many young men occupying Hatley Park. The ghost's reaction may have indeed been to shake one cadet awake, and drag him from her house. However, there may be more than one ghost in residence. A psychic who visited Hatley Park some years ago stated that there may have been a second presence there. She believed that Mrs. Dunsmuir's daughter, Eleanor, who died shortly after her mother, also haunted the family estate.

* * * * *

There is another brief Dunsmuir ghost story that may be mentioned here. James Dunsmuir's brother Alex, who lived in San Francisco, had a long history of alcohol abuse. Despite his wife Josephine's best efforts to keep him straight, Alex Dunsmuir continued drinking to excess, and by 1899, it was clear that his health was failing rapidly.

Dunsmuir's poor health was of course a considerable worry to his wife, but during the final months of his illness she had her own concern. She had been feeling unwell for some time and when she visited her doctor his diagnosis was most distressing — cancer. She was advised to have an operation as soon as possible, but because her husband was so ill, Mrs. Dunsmuir put off the ordeal. Alex Dunsmuir died on January 31, 1899, in New York.

Following the funeral, which was held in San Francisco, Mrs. Dunsmuir decided to postpone the operation for a little longer. She agreed to spend a few weeks with her brother-in-law, James Dunsmuir, and his family in Victoria. The Dunsmuirs were at the time still living at Burleith, their mansion overlooking the Gorge.

One day while standing by her bedroom window, the grieving widow was surprised to see the apparition of her late husband beside her. The ghost looked at her and said, "Josephine, pet, you'd better not stay too long or you'll be late for your operation."[10] Mrs. Dunsmuir quickly packed her bags and left for San Francisco where she underwent the operation.

The ghost, it seems, had no special prescient abilities. Even after the operation Josephine Dunsmuir's health continued to decline, and she died the following year.

MORE ON ROYAL ROADS

In 1995 the military college was closed by the federal government and a public educational institution — Royal Roads University — was opened. The kind of education provided at this institution has changed, but ghost stories continue to be part of campus lore.

In the summer of 2001, a plumber was working in a basement boiler room when a man passed by him. He might have thought little of the incident had not the visitor been bathed in a brilliant light. He had come from a closed-off section of the cellar that was not wired for electricity. As quickly as he appeared, the man vanished.[11]

BEBAN HOUSE: THE BOY WITH THE RED BALL

Although several entities have been seen and heard in Beban House, on Bowen Road in Nanaimo, the most tragic ghost appears to be that of a little boy, a child trapped in time and a destiny unfulfilled.

The mansion that Frank Beban built on 160 acres of rolling farmland three miles north of the centre of Nanaimo was indeed fitting for one of the province's leading timber barons. It was clearly to be a monument to a man who had made a fortune from the sale of British Columbia trees.

Beban was born in 1882 in the remote Waimes region of the Westlands district of New Zealand and emigrated to San Francisco around the turn of the 20th century. He worked in the mining towns of Nevada before coming to British Columbia about 1907. The newcomer competed in many running and wrestling meets in the province, and soon gained a reputation as an outstanding athlete. He began his financial empire as supplier of pit poles and crossbeams to the Dunsmuir coal-mining interests. Beban's operations expanded with the purchase of the Empire Lumber Company in 1927.

The rustic design, with broad front steps leading to a shaded front porch, and a porte-cochère side entrance, all contributed to the pleasing old-fashioned effect of Beban House. The exterior appearance, though, was misleading for Beban House was not a throwback to the past. It featured modern art-deco tile fireplaces, as well as something new in modern décor: pink plumbing fixtures — the first residence on Vancouver Island to use coloured porcelain to accent the bathrooms.

After the house was completed in 1930, Frank Beban, his wife Hannah, and their four children moved in. In 1944, he sold most of his interests and retired to his estate. Beban's passion was horse-racing, and he trained many of his thoroughbreds on the track behind his house. Although he was well known in both business and racing circles, Beban was a private man. Little of his personal life was ever made public.

By 1952, it was widely known in the Nanaimo area that Beban was in poor health. He nevertheless continued to be active as an owner and trainer of thoroughbred horses. On Tuesday, August 12, Beban had been in the city with friends. He appeared to be in good spirits, telling them that he had not felt so well in some time. That evening after he returned home, Beban spent a little while in his comfortable trophy room — the same room where he had so often enjoyed the company of longtime friends — before retiring to his bedroom on the main floor. Only Hannah Beban slept on the top floor, while the servants occupied quarters in the basement. Beban's children were married and living elsewhere. The next day, Beban was discovered dead in his room.

In 1953, the Beban estate was sold to the city of Nanaimo for use as a sports park, and new buildings were added. Little attention was paid to the house, though, and over the years it was used for a variety of purposes including equipment storage. It was not properly maintained, and by the early 1990s it was becoming evident to the city that Beban House would have to be torn down, before it rotted away. Although less than a hundred years old, it was one of the few remaining stately homes on the north side of Nanaimo and its destruction would have meant the loss of a style of architecture found nowhere else on Vancouver Island. In 1995, Beban House was declared a heritage site and, with the assistance of the senior governments, the city set about restoring it.

Prior to the building becoming the headquarters of Tourism Nanaimo in January 1997, the main floor served as a daycare centre. The operator of the facility was often surprised to hear stories from the preschoolers about a strangely dressed child playing with a red rubber ball. According to the children, their companion had long, black, tightly braided hair and wore a white nightgown. As children passed through the facility, their invisible playmate — invisible at least to adults — was sometimes the subject of their drawings, and the operator was struck by the similarity of the pictures.

While it was at first generally assumed that the ghost was a little girl, one of the children of the Bebans' Chinese servants, a young boy, had died in the house. As researchers have noted, braided hair would be in keeping with the appearance of a Chinese male during the first half of the last century.

Other events at Beban House point toward the presence of a child. Jack Bernard, Tourism Nanaimo's general manager, has been particularly aware of the happenings when he is alone in the building. "I've had incidents where I've heard footsteps running up and down the stairs."[12] The rapid movement and light patter seem to suggest the playful actions of a child, but Bernard has also heard creaks and groans from the stairway, as if the steps were protesting the weight of a heavier tread. In his office, which once was Frank Beban's trophy room, Jack Bernard has been plagued by a cupboard — formerly Beban's liquor cabinet — which won't stay shut. "I'll be at a meeting in my office, and any time during the meeting it opens all the way."[13]

For marketing executive Rosanna Tomkinson, a frequent and perplexing occurrence concerns a drawer in the file cabinet in her office. "The file cabinet is tilted toward the wall," Tomkinson explained, "so there's no way these drawers pull out on their own. But one will just open."[14]

While the sound of measured footsteps is the most frequent ghostly manifestation, other noises are sometimes associated

Beban House, now the headquarters of Tourism Nanaimo, has some of the most active ghosts north of Victoria. (COURTESY OF D. M. BELYK)

with the haunting of Beban House. One strange occurrence took place in the fall of 2000. An organization sharing space in Beban House is the United Way Campaign, which has an office on the second floor. Tomkinson came to work one morning and began tidying up the large room that had once been the kitchen. As she washed some dishes she was aware of the clinking of teacups and the sound of women's voices. She assumed that the noises came from the United Way workers who must have arrived early and were having tea upstairs. She thought little of the incident until she heard a door open: the United Way volunteers had just arrived. Tomkinson suddenly realized that these women could not have produced the sounds of teacups and light chatter. Until they arrived, she had been the only living person in Beban House.

Some years earlier, another member of the Tourism Nanaimo staff was in her office when she heard someone yelling. While it was unclear whether the voice was male or female, it certainly was loud. The sound was confined to her office. Other people in the building heard nothing.

Like other haunted buildings, Beban House becomes most active after a period when few people have been in the facility. Tourism Nanaimo was closed to the public between Christmas 2000 and New Year's Day 2001. During this time Tomkinson had the task of moving an old chandelier, which had been stored in the basement boiler room, to the city's museum. Because the object was heavy, she had asked her husband to help her. As she recalled, "I was walking over to it and was just going to pick it up when someone started stomping on the floor."[15] The area above them had been Frank Beban's bedroom, the room where he died.

Another room that seems particularly active is the master bedroom on the second floor. One day in late 1999, before the United Way had taken over the room as an office, one of the staff saw that there was a light burning in the apparently empty office. Tomkinson climbed the stairs from her office to the second floor and unlocked the door. All the lights were off, "but the room was ice cold." Other people have driven past the house during the night and reported a glow coming from the master bedroom, but when the room was examined the next day no light had been left on.

The boiler room and the bleak quarters once used by the Bebans' Chinese servants in the basement are areas that leave many people feeling uncomfortable. One psychic, whose child attended the daycare in the 1990s, toured the building and noted that the boiler room was a very unpleasant place. She had difficulty breathing and felt she had to leave. The psychic never asked to see the basement again.

Another upstairs room is used by the RCMP as a community policing office, and constables frequently arrive at night to catch up on their paperwork. One officer, finished for the night, was locking his door when he saw a woman standing in front of the master bedroom. When he blinked and looked again the figure was gone. The constable did not provide a description of the person he so briefly glimpsed.

Early in 2001, a staff member arrived at work and checked her voice mail. She noted a message dated 11:20 AM the previous night. There was nothing on the tape but a noise that sounded like someone was walking heavily across the floor. The hollow stomping sound seemed particularly eerie. In Rosanna Tomkinson's opinion, it was not an outside phone call. "I feel [the recording] was coming from within the house."[16]

There have been many other incidents. During the time when the second floor was vacant, a staff member working on the main floor was suddenly aware of the sound of water running. "We checked the bathrooms downstairs," Tomkinson recalled, "and then went upstairs. And there was water running in the sink in the bathroom. There was nobody up there." Often the staff has heard the sound of doors opening and closing at times when the entrances are locked.

General Manager Jack Bernard has experienced many unexplained events but is not deterred by them. The staff members have also adapted well to their unseen visitors, although with few exceptions, no one is prepared to remain there alone in the evening. When it comes to ghosts — even the harmless entities that haunt Beban House — it may be better to keep one's distance.

Haunted Houses

THE WILLIAMS STREET HAUNTING: PORTRAIT OF A GHOST

Haunted portraits are a theme of many ghost stories. For some reason, ghosts appear to have a particular affinity for such works of art. Yet the story of one unusual British Columbia picture is even stranger than other portrait tales. The picture in question here is not entirely the work of a living person — it is said that the finishing touches were supplied by a ghost.

In the mid-1960s, the huge three-storey structure on Chilliwack's Williams Street could easily have been mistaken for the set of a Gothic horror movie, but the old house wasn't a Hollywood prop; it was entirely real, and in the winter of 1965 it became home to Douglas and Hetty Fredrickson and their family.

The big house was just right for a large family — the Fredricksons had five children — but there was another advantage as well. The old house had character of the kind that would inspire an artist like Mrs. Fredrickson. It was the perfect place for the new owner to set up her studio. However, as the Fredricksons were about to discover, the house's "character" went beyond providing the artist with inspiration.

Mrs. Fredrickson had not been in the house long when it became apparent to her that something was wrong. The couple intended to use one of the large upstairs bedrooms which overlooked Williams Street for guests, but it was not possible. This room seemed to be the centre of a haunting.

At night footsteps would be heard on the stairs leading to the upper floor. The new owners would, of course, check through the house, but there was never anyone there. When Mrs. Fredrickson examined the guest bedroom the following morning, dresser drawers which she made sure were closed the previous night would be open, while the heavy old iron bedstead would have been moved about the room. The bed actually seemed to be restless, moving night after night until it finally found the right location under a window.

There were other incidents that were frightening, like the sound of breathing in an apparently empty room and, strangely, the smell of perfume. The Fredricksons would suddenly be aware that perfume was permeating the room.

In the beginning, at least, Mrs. Fredrickson was more puzzled than frightened. "I am not afraid," she remarked, "but I would like to find a logical explanation."[1] The problem was that as far as she could determine, there simply wasn't any rational interpretation. Moreover, something else was happening which Mrs. Fredrickson found extremely distressing. Soon after moving into the house, she began having a terrible recurring nightmare. Night after night she had the same dream: the body of a woman lying on the floor of the hall upstairs. "She is sort of mummified and she has a red dress on with yellow flowers, a cheap cotton dress, and she is terrified," explained Mrs. Fredrickson.[2]

Mrs. Fredrickson found the haunting, combined with her recurring dream, very upsetting. However, she was not without considerable personal fortitude, and after putting up with the disturbances for five months, Mrs. Fredrickson was determined to get to the bottom of the mystery. She undertook a two-step plan against the ghost. First, she would dig into the history of the house to discover if any tragic event had occurred there, particularly something involving a woman. "I intend to find out if someone has been living here with this dress on," she told reporters, "because I can describe it absolutely."

Second, she prepared to meet the ghost on its own turf. Beginning the last week in May 1966, Mrs. Fredrickson decided to wait up for the ghost. Taking her sketch pad, a pencil and a candle to the "haunted" spare bedroom, she planned to sit all night until the ghost appeared. Then she would draw its picture. Why draw its picture? As an artist, Mrs. Fredrickson became convinced that simply rendering its likeness on paper or canvas would rid the house of the spectre.

For two nights nothing untoward happened. On the third night Mrs. Fredrickson became aware of something. Near the window she saw what she described as "a sort of light," but the misty luminescence took on no clear definition. "It looked like a cloudy figure," she later recalled. "It was the shape of a human being, but no details, no face." As she stared at the glowing shape before her, Mrs. Fredrickson wondered if it was no more than a product of her imagination. "I closed my eyes and opened them and it was still there. I didn't dare get up. When it went, it just disappeared." The ghost was more than a visual experience. Soon after it had gone, she was aware of something pleasant in the air. "I could definitely smell perfume."

Although for her purposes, Mrs. Fredrickson's experience with the ghost was unsatisfactory — she was not able to see the features of the apparition clearly — she was determined to render the image on canvas. She decided to combine the faceless form of the ghost with the image of the dead girl in the floral print dress from her dream but she had trouble "capturing" the elusive ghost on canvas. In the end, to signify her difficulty with the project, Mrs. Fredrickson left half the head uncompleted, putting in the eye on only one side of the face. The artist spent a number of days working on the portrait and when it was done, she had produced a very large canvas — it measured about four feet by six feet — of the "ghost."

About a week after painting the picture, Mrs. Fredrickson became aware that, like the portrait in Oscar Wilde's famous novel, *The Picture of Dorian Gray*, it was beginning to change on its own. However, unlike the work in the Wilde allegory, the picture was recasting not the age of the subject, but its sex. "The woman's portrait is changing to that of a man," she told the reporters who

The Fredrickson house. (COURTESY OF HETTY FREDRICKSON)

were now beginning to take a considerable interest in the story. "I haven't touched the painting but it is gradually changing."[3]

It was, Mrs. Fredrickson maintained, definitely not the face she had painted earlier. The details on the uncompleted side of the face were beginning to fill in on their own and the changes were quite dramatic. The dark side of the face lightened considerably, and took on an eyelid and a nostril, as well as an outline of the cheek. The painted side of the face changed also. What appeared to be a very thin moustache was visible under the nose, while heavier lines of shadow hardened the face. The change in the portrait was strange because Mrs. Fredrickson had painted the face of the woman she saw so vividly in her dreams. The person in the cotton print dress lying on the hall floor was obviously not a man.

About the same time as she discovered the alterations to her painting, Mrs. Fredrickson heard several rumours about the history of the house. One story she was told concerned an old man who had committed suicide in or near the house a number of years earlier.

Apparently who he was, or why he had taken his own life, was not known at the time, but as far as Mrs. Fredrickson was concerned, it did reveal that the old house had a violent history. Another rumour, about a woman who was supposedly murdered and bricked up in a chimney, seemed to strike a responsive chord with the artist. This could explain the woman in the print dress in her dreams. However, the Fredricksons came to the conclusion that the rumour was too fantastic to be true. Terrible things like that just didn't happen in quiet little farming communities in the Fraser Valley.

The Fredricksons began a painstaking search through the old house for the remains of an old chimney. The house, the couple soon discovered, was full of surprises. After removing a wall of panelling in the attic, they found a boarded-up door, which led to the old-fashioned turret room visible from the road. While the room was found to contain only insulation and dust, Mrs. Fredrickson felt strongly that it was the setting of her terrible dreams, the place where the body of the young woman lay on the floor. Why this room was sealed off so completely from the rest of the house was not known.

On June 1, 1966, two reporters from the Vancouver *Sun* and a friend arranged with Mrs. Fredrickson to spend the night in the "haunted" bedroom. However, with the exception of the mysterious relocation of a roll of linoleum and some noise in the hall, the trio observed nothing strange. The ghost watch was regarded as a failure.

Mrs. Fredrickson had hoped that publicity would bring forward someone who could solve the mystery of what was happening at the old house, but the many newspaper articles seemed to provoke only considerable public speculation regarding the presence or absence of the Williams Street ghost. During the first few weeks in June "Hetty's ghost" became a popular topic in British Columbia.

On June 3, 1966, the Vancouver *Sun* published an interview with the previous owner of the Williams Street house, Mrs. Margaret Lindhout. The lady had very definite views regarding Mrs. Fredrickson and her ghost, claiming that her son had slept in the "haunted bedroom" for four years without experiencing anything unusual. While she did confirm that an old man had committed suicide in the slough at the back of the house, as far as the ghost was concerned, Mrs. Lindhout was firm. "It is all a lot of baloney," she concluded.[4] Mrs. Fredrickson, however, was equally convinced of what she had seen and heard in the house. The picture continued to change — Mrs. Fredrickson maintained that the moustache which had only lately appeared, was now gradually disappearing and the faint outline of a beard was beginning to emerge.

Mrs. Fredrickson had been in touch with Professor Geoffrey Riddehough of the University of British Columbia. The professor was a member of Britain's well-respected Society for Psychical Research. She arranged to show him her picture, but if reports in the press were any indication, the professor was more concerned with understanding the nature of the phenomena which may have been in the Chilliwack house than with bringing an end to the disturbances themselves. Professor Riddehough said only that he would make a study of the incident later, but nothing more was heard from him.

Then Mrs. Fredrickson announced that she would hold a seance the following Sunday to contact the spirit in her house. She had invited a clairvoyant to attend. In addition, she invited local school children accompanied by their parents to tour the house. Mrs. Fredrickson had been apprised of some of the gruesome stories concerning the "ghost picture" that were being told among the children at Chilliwack schools, and she wanted them to see for themselves that there was nothing horrible at the house. Her plan, unfortunately, turned out to be entirely too successful.

On Sunday, June 5, an estimated 700 sightseers besieged the Fredrickson house. At its height, the line of visitors extended well into the street, and the stairs leading to the front door collapsed under the weight of those waiting to be admitted. "I didn't want all the children of Chilliwack having nightmares, so I told their school they could see for themselves that there is nothing horrific about the place," an exhausted Mrs. Fredrickson explained. "But more grown-ups turned up than children. You wouldn't believe it."[5] The crowds ended any hope of holding a seance, and the clairvoyant went home early.

That Sunday was only the beginning. For the next few weeks the house was one of the province's greatest tourist attractions. The Fredricksons could do nothing but watch the hundreds of people stream past. "Some of them," observed a bewildered Mrs. Fredrickson, "must have expected the ghost to ask if they wanted tea or coffee or something."[6] By now the story of the ghost picture had been circulated beyond the boundaries of the province. A constant stream of cars, many with American licence plates, drove past the house. Mrs. Fredrickson posted "no trespassing" signs and

Hetty Fredrickson's portrait of the ghost. (COURTESY OF HETTY FREDRICKSON)

made a public appeal that the family's right to privacy should be respected. However, the cars continued to come, and it was estimated that 200 cars a day were driving by the "ghost house."

The almost constant distraction of the crowds of visitors did not, however, dampen the activities of the ghost. "It even shows up afternoons now and will spend several hours opening and closing bureau drawers in an unused bedroom," Mrs. Fredrickson wearily observed.[7] By the end of June, only about a month after the first account of the Chilliwack ghost had reached the province's major newspapers, Mrs. Fredrickson had had enough. Being at the centre of the ghost story was hard on the entire family.

"I never wanted to turn my house into a tourist attraction," a very frustrated Mrs. Fredrickson told a reporter for the Vancouver *Daily Province*. "You would think that after a while interest would die down."[8] Not long after that interview the Fredricksons admitted defeat. Mrs. Fredrickson had hoped to determine what was happening at the house. She had failed, but the streams of visitors were turning her life, and the lives of other members of her family, into a nightmare. The Fredricksons finally closed their doors and moved to Vancouver Island. In the late 1960s, Mrs. Fredrickson lent the now-famous haunted picture to a charity project associated with the Vancouver radio station CKNW, where it became part of the "Haunted House" exhibit at the Pacific National Exhibition. During the time it was on display, the painting was seen by thousands of fair visitors.

While it is uncertain whether the picture really changed or not, it is clear that the mood of near-hysteria generated by the occurrences in the house prevented an objective evaluation of the painting. During the time when interest in the picture was at its height, the paint on the portrait had been "tested" so much by the curious public that it was being worn off.

Those who were sceptical of the haunting seemed to be supported by the fact that the Fredrickson ghost story came to an end immediately after the family left. The house stayed vacant for some time and the property was repeatedly vandalized — so badly that even a tub was stolen from a bathroom. Finally in 1968,

Hetty Fredrickson, around the time of the haunting. (COURTESY OF HETTY FREDRICKSON)

Mrs. Fredrickson arranged for a group of 12 musicians to move into the house. In exchange for free rent the young men took care of upkeep and small repairs. During their stay, the musicians reported seeing no ghosts. Subsequently the house was sold and rented out to a series of tenants.

Then, in the spring of 1972 another family moved in: a man, his wife and eight children. The wife (who, after the Fredrickson fiasco, didn't want to have her name mentioned in the media) complained about doors that would bang when no one was around and how the thermostat would be turned up to 80 degrees. One of the most striking things about the ghost or ghosts (the family believed there were three distinct entities "living" there) was that their dog, Lucky, seemed to be so afraid during these episodes. Normally he was not frightened by anything, but when doors slammed shut, Lucky could be found shaking and cowering in a corner. Very frightening, also, was the fact that, like Mrs. Fredrickson, the children of the Williams Street house were beginning to suffer from terrible nightmares.

There were now rumours of other mysterious incidents. Some people who had briefly occupied the house obtained other accommodation and moved out. When they returned to pick up the last of their things, they said that they saw, "something like a shadow moving back and forth."[9] When a delivery woman for one of the department stores pulled up in front of the house to deliver a package, a woman carrying a baby suddenly appeared on the porch. The delivery woman could tell that these two were not living beings. She eventually dropped the package on the sidewalk and ran away.

In 1973 the old house was again up for sale. Reporters from the Vancouver newspapers tried to contact the owner of the house, James Kipp, to find out why the house was being sold, but they had no success. He was not available for comment. Several years later fire broke out in the basement, and the house was destroyed.

Some time after she had moved away from Williams Street, Mrs. Fredrickson recalled that at the height of the haunting craze, she was afraid to even sweep her porch with her broom. As she admitted sadly, it was simply not wise to be caught with a broom in her hand — it would be impossible to know what one of the many little children, who always seemed to be waiting around outside the house, might imagine and say.

* * * * *

Sometimes it is relatively easy to discover the details of a haunting. In the case of Tod House, for example, Colonel and Mrs. Evans spent many years in the house, and thus were able to recall many unusual happenings there. Also, although they at first didn't believe in ghosts, they were careful and credible observers and were prepared to acknowledge what they had witnessed.

Unfortunately for those interested in such phenomena, well-documented hauntings of this kind are rare. Frequently, none of the inhabitants of a haunted house stay there long. Because resident ghosts tend to bring property values down, many owners will quietly sell the dwelling and move on, rather than acknowledge the truth. At other times, although people may be willing to report strange goings-on to the press, they stipulate that their address is not to be made public. While one can sympathize with the plight of these people, concealing the location makes follow-up difficult or impossible. On some occasions, too, the details of the haunting are not reported until years after the event and by that time the witnesses, now living somewhere else, have only a limited recollection of what occurred.

The following stories can be classified as minor hauntings, not because the ghost is any less interesting, but because the history of the occurrences is too limited.

Oscar's Tricks

When their friends George and Sandy first suggested it, Anne Houseman and her husband, Jim, thought the idea was great. George was supervising a major construction project in northern British Columbia and the couple would be gone almost two years. In the meantime, George and Sandy would let the Housemans stay in their house rent-free. Although the house on East Second Avenue in Vancouver wasn't large, it would suit the two of them. Moreover, for Anne and Jim, who hoped one day to purchase their own home, this would be a chance to save some money. "There's just one slight hitch," Sandy admitted. "We've got a ghost here."[10]

It was a late December evening in 1977 when the two couples were sitting in the front room talking. The ghost — Sandy called the presence "Oscar" — was quite harmless, and should cause no difficulty. Sandy explained that Oscar seemed to enjoy entertaining the couple's children, and in the morning she would hear them laughing at the antics of the ghost.

Anne Houseman was not particularly frightened by the prospect of a ghost in the house, while her husband simply didn't believe in the supernatural. (He was to change his mind later, however.) The fact that their friends believed the house was haunted would certainly not dissuade the Housemans from moving in.

"By the way," Sandy continued, "Oscar is around now. He keeps turning off the red Christmas lights." Anne looked at the Christmas tree which was next to her chair. One of the red lights was indeed out. She reached down and gave it several turns. The light came on. Obviously it was not defective; it had simply been loosened. Several minutes later she turned around to look at the tree. All the Christmas lights were on except one: another red bulb had somehow become loose in its socket.

Before the Housemans moved in, their friends told them that they had purchased the house from an elderly couple. The couple had not mentioned anything about a resident ghost, but that would not be surprising; ghosts are not usually regarded as positive selling features. The dwelling was obviously old, dating from around 1900. There had probably been many owners during the years and it was impossible to tell when the phenomenon originated.

The Housemans moved into the house in January 1978, and it did not take long for Oscar to make his presence known. The couple was sound asleep in the early hours of the morning when a shrill noise suddenly erupted from the kitchen. It was the whistling tea kettle that had been standing quietly on the stove when they went to bed hours earlier. There was no way it could have suddenly boiled without someone turning up the gas under it.

"Stop it, Oscar," Jim called out humorously. To the couple's surprise, the sound abruptly stopped. When Jim and Anne went into the kitchen to investigate, they found that the stove was only operating on its pilot lights, and the tea kettle was stone cold. After that, when Oscar was performing similar tricks, Jim would simply call out for him to stop, and the disturbances would cease as abruptly as they had begun.

The house was very small and space was at a premium. At one time the attic had been renovated and an extra bedroom added. It was from this room that Anne would hear the noises. They sounded as if someone was wrecking the place — things falling, furniture being dragged across the floor — but when she went to check, the room was just as it had been left, with nothing out of place.

On another occasion the couple was in bed when Anne heard a racket from the bathroom. It sounded as if her large metal comb had fallen into the sink and clattered around. She asked her husband to go into the bathroom and see what had happened; to his surprise the comb had not fallen into the sink. Instead, it stood where it usually was: propped up against a towel rack.

At times, however, Oscar did move things. Late one evening Anne was catching up on her vacuuming before her husband came home. In the living room she cleaned the area around the hearth where she kept an ornamental copper kettle. She had turned off the vacuum cleaner and left the room when she heard a scraping sound, as though someone was dragging the kettle along the hearth. Sure enough, the kettle had been moved from its usual place on one end of the hearth — the spot where she had seen it only minutes before — and set at the opposite side.

One of Oscar's more common tricks was to play with a fireplace poker. There were a number of tools beside the fireplace but he seemed to favour the poker. The Housemans would watch it swing back and forth for 15 or 20 minutes without stopping. Jim checked in the area of the fireplace for drafts, but he could never find anything to account for the action of the iron.

One of the strangest incidents occurred when Jim was away at a convention and Anne was home alone. She was lying in bed when she was suddenly aware of footsteps outside her door, but the sound somehow seemed to be muffled. She lay awake listening to the noises when suddenly she was aware of movement in the room. The quilt she had thrown over herself was moving: an unseen hand was tucking her in.

Like many similar hauntings, both Housemans were aware of sudden, very localized, drops in temperature. Although the incidents seemed to happen more frequently downstairs than upstairs, no specific room was affected, only certain spots. By stepping only a foot away they would suddenly feel warmer.

Oscar remained with the Housemans until they moved into their own home 18 months later. As far as is known he continues his pleasant haunt of the East Vancouver house.

THE SNORING GHOST

If we accept the "recording theory" to explain the activity of most ghosts, then the record almost always involves an important moment in a person's life. Often what is recorded is the last few moments of life, before the individual meets a violent death. Thus we see a victim seconds before he puts a revolver to his head, or is stabbed, strangled or poisoned by an unkind lover. This is not surprising because these may be the most important minutes in any person's life (or death). While this seems sensible enough, what can be said about a house haunted by someone snoring? The sounds of someone's last snore hardly seem important enough to be replayed through the years, but one such case occurred about the beginning of the First World War.

Margery Wighton was 15 when her father sold the family's Okanagan fruit farm and moved to a remote area on Vancouver Island. Margery's father intended to start a chicken farm on the 12 acres of uncleared land the family had purchased, but there was a problem. Their new home was still under construction. It would be about eight weeks before they could move into their home and in the meantime they needed a place to stay.

The difficulty was overcome when a local farmer offered them a shack which stood vacant on his property. The small dwelling looked far from inviting, half-hidden as it was under a wall of tall fir trees and thick underbrush. Not far from the front door the ground suddenly fell away into a deep ravine, which increased the feeling of isolation and heaviness. Inside, the cabin didn't make the new residents feel much brighter: it was a very rudely constructed affair with a small kitchen and living room and two small bedrooms upstairs. However, it was early summer, and the house was pleasantly cool in the heat. Moreover, since Margery and her parents would have to endure this shack for only a short time, everyone agreed to make the best of it.

The family spent the first few days at the site of their new home, overseeing construction. By the time they returned home and had supper, everyone was very tired and fell asleep almost immediately. About nine o'clock on the third night, Margery retired to bed as usual, leaving her father sitting in a chair in the front room, reading a book. Before she went to sleep, however, her mother came into the room and sat on the bed discussing several matters with her daughter. Abruptly, the older woman stopped in mid-sentence. They both listened to the very familiar and comfortable sound of someone snoring. The noise was very loud and sounded very close to where they were sitting on the bed.

"Daddy must be tired," Margery's mother remarked.[11]

By now the noise had intrigued both women. Instead of going to sleep Margery went downstairs with her mother. In the front room they found Margery's father sitting reading.

"I thought you were asleep," his wife said. "We heard you snoring."

"You must both be mad," he replied indignantly. "I'm reading a good book."

When the women had again climbed the stairs, they stopped and listened. The snoring could still be heard. Margery's mother was convinced that her husband was playing some sort of trick on them. Both women quietly crept downstairs, thinking they would catch him in the act of pretending to snore. What they found instead was the man sitting in his chair, deeply engrossed in his book. He said, "If you two think this is awfully amusing, I don't."

Now they were thoroughly perplexed. They explained the situation to Margery's father, and reluctantly he agreed to check upstairs; as soon as they reached Margery's room, the snoring could be heard again.

Now it was Margery's father's turn to be puzzled. "There's someone here," he said. "But where?" Except for the bed and a table, the room was empty. The family searched the upper floor completely but nothing could be found to account for the strange sounds. No snoring could be heard outside the doorway to that one bedroom. Since nothing could be found inside the house, it seemed logical to conclude that the noise arose outside. The three family members trudged outside and listened, but no snoring could be heard. Everything outside was in fact dead still.

The snore had now upset the entire family. Margery's father vowed not to go to sleep until he had "laid the ghost." Margery went to bed but tossed and turned all night. In the morning her father was no closer to a solution to the mystery. "I'm damned if I can stand it," he admitted. The previous night he had spent hours trying to locate the noise; he still hadn't turned up anything.

The following day he picked up the owner of the house, and together the two men raked the roof. However, because the house was not insulated or built upon a proper foundation there was really no place to conceal whatever or whoever was making the maddening snoring sound.

When evening had fallen their landlord returned to see if they were again troubled by the noise. They were. "Night after night," Mrs. Wighton noted later, "our 'snorer' enjoyed his slumbers while we had little rest." Neighbours suggested all kinds of causes: chipmunks, spiders, owls, deer and even Indian tom-toms. There was one thing wrong with all these "solutions," however: the only place the sound could be heard was in that one small bedroom.

The family accommodated the snoring as best they could. Margery and her mother used the larger bedroom; her father slept downstairs. The ghost snorer was given the small bedroom to itself. Life went on for everyone, just about as usual. One day a Vancouver architect, Clem Webb, arrived for a visit. Webb was a good friend of Margery's parents and they all looked forward to his arrival. It would also give them a chance to show off their haunted bedroom. With a guest staying over, the room would be pressed into service. Everyone waited in the bedroom for the snorer to begin his nightly session, but nothing happened. For the first time in six weeks the room was not filled with the sound of snoring. Webb was credited with "laying the ghost" at last.

Not long after Webb's visit, the family moved into their new home, and the snoring incident was almost forgotten. A year later, the owner of the shack ordered a new car from a Vancouver dealer. In due course the vehicle was delivered, but the farmer, never having driven before, thought it wise for the delivery man to stay around a few days and give him driving lessons. This was agreed to, but because the farmer lacked space in his house, the man had to sleep in the shack.

Around midnight the farmer was awakened by the delivery man. He was shaking all over. "The place is haunted," the man swore, and went on to tell a frightening story.[12] It seems he had locked up the house and prepared for an early night's sleep in the small upstairs bedroom when he heard either the front or back door open. Someone, he claimed, came in, climbed the stairs, dropped his boots in the bedroom, and almost immediately fell asleep, snoring loudly. After searching the place from one end to the other, the man maintained, he could see no one in the house. The man would have no more to do with that haunted shack. He packed his bag and left for Vancouver, leaving the farmer to learn to drive as best he could.

There is a possible explanation for the snoring. When someone is close to death, it is not uncommon for his or her breathing to become laboured. The condition is called "rales" and it can sound just like somebody snoring. The "snoring" then could be simply an at-the-time-of-death incident which for some reason was played back like a tape recorder in the small bedroom for years after the actual occurrence.

A FAMILY OF GHOSTS

At the time it was built, the old house was probably one of Victoria's finest, but when John West bought it in 1969, it had fallen into disrepair. While the house had been empty, vandals had broken doors, smashed windows and removed most of the antique doorknobs. The grass in the front yard was knee deep and the trees around the property desperately needed pruning.

However, the large house had obviously been magnificent in its day. The two fireplaces, one in the living room and the other in the dining room, were still bordered by beautiful mantels of carved solid oak. West estimated it had been built around the turn of the 20th century. It would be the kind of place to which former residents could become very attached — even to the point of staying on beyond the grave. At least that's what the tenants who moved in firmly believed. They were convinced that the house was haunted, and not by a single entity, but by a whole family of ghosts which even included an invisible cat. Within weeks of moving in, the people who shared the old house were severely frightened by the ghostly goings-on.

The house was rented in September 1969 to a young couple from Ontario, Brent and Jan Lowell (not their real names), who in turn took in boarders, Gilles from Montreal and Bob from New York. In addition, an area upstairs was rented as a day studio by a young artist. All the tenants believed that the house was haunted by very active ghosts. "There's an old man," Jan Lowell began. "We believe him to be an old man by the way he walks …. He lives upstairs in the front room. He walks halfway down the stairs, stops and then goes back to his room."[13]

There were other ghosts as well. The woman and the baby were particularly chilling because people don't usually think of ghosts as being mothers with infants. "We can hear the baby cry," Jan continued. "The woman talks, but we've never been able to make out any words. It is as if she is comforting the baby."

Then there were the cat stories. Bob related one incident concerning a cat that no one could see:

> We were in the front living room when the cat came down. We could hear it padding down the stairs. It stopped at the hallway door, let out a meow. Then there seemed to be footsteps across the living room and it jumped on the fireplace mantel and began to meow again. [Three] of us were in the same room, but [we] couldn't see anything.

Immediately, all three decided it was time to leave the room. The cat had also been heard scratching on the kitchen window, apparently to be let in. "I didn't believe in ghosts," Bob admitted, "not until I moved into this house."

On another occasion Bob and five friends entered the kitchen to find broken glass covering the floor. They were just going to clean up the mess when suddenly they were aware of the sound of someone walking close by. The footsteps, Bob noted, "came into the kitchen, made a terrible racket. It also sounded as if someone dropped a broom." Bob and his visitors made a hasty exit from the kitchen.

Most of those living in the house watched various doors open and shut without human assistance. "Someone might say it is because the house is settling," Brent observed. "But look at the house. It's built on a rock, with a rock and cement foundation."

The tenants were not alone in what they felt about the house. Brent claimed that once their sceptical friends had had an opportunity to experience the house, "Every one changed his view." Even John West, the owner, had a feeling that there was something creepy about the place. While renovating the structure, he became aware of one room with a cold drafty spot, where there was no place for air to get in.

The fact that the presences seemed more noticeable during the daytime, when the owner was working on the house, makes this haunting a little different from most cases. Usually, unexplained phenomena occur during the night. These ghosts, however, exhibited a marked preference for the afternoon, and were never heard during the evening or night hours.

Unlike other tenants who had quickly moved on, the young couple and their boarders stayed, even in the face of the strange happenings in the house. It was Bob's opinion that a person could adjust to almost anything. "It's weird," he noted, "I feel safe and secure most of the time. Then, at times when I'm alone, I get the feeling that I'm not supposed to be there. I drop whatever I'm doing and walk out."

It has been 30 years since the ghosts frightened the young tenants of the old Victoria house. While the exact location of the house was not mentioned at the time the haunting was reported, several Victoria ghost sleuths think it stood on Quadra Street. If they are right, the house was torn down some time ago to make way for a church.

* * * * *

Interestingly, there is another apparently haunted house in Victoria which has recently met the wrecker's ball. This house, built around the turn of the 20th century, was an eerie old place completely surrounded by thorn bushes. The bushes made everything more spooky because they seemed to be constantly scratching against the sides of the house — even when it wasn't windy.

In 1977, when Rick Johnston moved into the old house on Vernon Street, the former tenants, who were moving out the last of their belongings, yelled, "Take good care of our friend."[14] He, of course, didn't know what they meant, but he soon found out.

Johnston had not been in the house long when one night he and a friend were sitting in the living room. Suddenly an ashtray which had been on one end of the coffee table slid the entire length of the table and fell to the floor. Neither man was anywhere near the ashtray at the time. Another strange occurrence concerned Johnston's bedroom door. It was his habit to close his door when he retired for the night. However, after living in the house about two weeks he began to notice that when he got up in the morning, the door would be open.

Whatever was haunting the old house seemed to take particular pleasure in playing with the old ringer washer in the basement. "I'd be sitting there at night and I'd listen and it would be on," he recalled. "I would go down and turn it off and unplug it. But when I got up in the morning it would be on again."

There were other incidents as well. The ghost apparently liked heat. When Johnston returned from work the thermostat would frequently be turned "up as high as it would go." Johnston found the incidents so unsettling he finally moved out of the house. Not long afterwards, the house was torn down to make way for a new supermarket.

A Creepy Old Haunt

Like Victoria, the old city of New Westminster on the mainland seems to have a large number of ghosts. One apparently well-haunted residence is the house owned by Jim and Lou Dodds. It is a huge, 13-room structure, built almost a hundred years ago, when New Westminster was still the major city on the mainland and Vancouver only a young upstart. When the Dodds family moved in in 1967, the house had long fallen on hard times and was in need of considerable repair. Dodds, a carpenter, spent much of his free time renovating it.

The Doddses had been living in the house about two years when the first incident happened. A family friend who was staying with them was sleeping in one of the bedrooms when he awoke to catch, out of the corner of his eye, the image of a man in the room. The figure was standing by the window staring off into the night. The man seemed middle-aged, but the clothes he was wearing were all wrong. The hat and long coat were clearly from an earlier time.

When the guest turned his head to gain a better look at the stranger, the figure immediately vanished. He was apparently not the only one who witnessed the spectre. Raggs, the family dog, was found some time later hiding beneath the bed. The unfortunate pet had clearly seen something that frightened it very much.

Jim Dodds also had a strange experience one night, when he checked the house before retiring for bed. Everything on the ground floor seemed perfectly normal, so he switched off the lights and turned toward the staircase. When he reached the foot of the stairs, he put his hand on the newel post. Suddenly he was aware of a strange sensation. He felt as though someone in the darkness had taken his hand. When he moved up the stairs the mysterious hand-holder continued to accompany him. "I didn't know what to think," he said later. "I wasn't scared, but [the feeling] was very real."[15] Finally, he was forced to shake his hand free.

At night, when Mrs. Dodds was up late working around the house, she felt a presence, "like a whirlwind around me," and the room she was in suddenly turned icy cold. Mrs. Dodds also saw, on the stairs, what she described as "the shadow of a woman ... wearing a long dress."

There was also the light switch in the upstairs bathroom. The switch, Dodds explained, was one of the old-fashioned spring-loaded types: it took considerable force to turn it off or on. Sometimes, however, when the entire family was downstairs, that upstairs switch would be heard clicking on and off.

Following the death of his wife in September 1988, Dodds continued to note strange goings-on in the house. Once, after he had retired for the night, he saw a white smokey shape appear just above his bed. The wispy form, he recalled later, "seemed to give off a faint glow."[16] At first he was frightened, but then it occurred to him that there was nothing in the house to harm him. He turned over and went to sleep.

FOOTSTEPS

In 1960, the Hilton family rented an unusual old house in White Rock. It came with the sound of distinctive footsteps creeping around the upstairs of the house. There was never anyone to be seen, but there was certainly something to be heard, and the family found these strange happenings disturbing.

The footsteps had been heard by those outside the immediate family as well. Henry Hilton explained that over one Easter weekend his brother, Markland, and his wife visited them from Saskatchewan. This was not Markland's first visit to the White Rock house — he and his wife had been there three times before. Previously he had scoffed at the stories of the phantom footsteps but during this particular visit, the couple spent the night in one of the upstairs bedrooms.

The next morning, when Markland Hilton came downstairs, he looked pale and shaken. He stated that some time after midnight, he suddenly awoke to hear the sound of footsteps: someone was shuffling along the hallway just outside his bedroom. Then the footsteps seemed to turn into the room he and his wife were occupying. Markland asked who was there but he received no answer. The footsteps just kept on coming slowly. By then Markland was quite distressed. Although not a particularly religious man, he felt compelled to challenge the approaching steps: "In the name of the Father, Son, and Holy Ghost."[17] Only then did the sound suddenly halt. Markland's wife heard the frightening noise as well and from then on she refused to go to the upstairs rooms unless someone went with her.

There might be several explanations for the strange noises. The Hiltons are a large family. (At the time when the sounds were reported in the press in 1963, Henry and Mary Hilton had eight children ranging in age from an infant to 18 years old.) Could the sounds have been made by one of the children? Not according to Mrs. Hilton who heard the footsteps in the afternoon when she was alone in the house. When the noises were heard, members of the family would do quick checks of the house, but nothing was ever discovered that would account for the sounds.

The house was also inspected thoroughly for possible causes of the phenomena. Tree branches striking the roof were ruled out and so were loose electric or telephone wires. Even more striking evidence against the "natural cause theory" was the fact that the noises sounded so clearly like shuffling footsteps. The Hiltons had lived in the house long enough to tell the difference between natural and unnatural noises, and as far as they were concerned it was clear that the footsteps defied simple explanation.

As often happens, Mr. and Mrs. Hilton became used to the noises during the three years they lived in the White Rock house. After all, whatever it was never did anyone any harm. However, some of the younger children never became accustomed to the strange goings-on, and one little boy refused to go upstairs by himself.

TWISTS IN TIME

On the day her grandmother died in 1972, 11-year-old Angela Bremner (a pseudonym) had been staying in the Kootenays. Although the family was saddened by their loss, the older woman's death was not a surprise; she had been in poor health for years and was confined to a wheelchair. Angela would later believe that the death was partly the result of abuse because she remembered her grandmother using cosmetics to cover up the bruises on her body.

Soon after her grandmother's death, Angela began to experience a deeply disturbing nightmare. It would also prove to be a harbinger of her future. The same dream occurred about six times a year. Afterwards she would awaken in a panicky cold sweat. She described the experience:

> I am walking up a long driveway. There's big trees on both sides and from a branch in a tree there appears a very small — about three feet, six [inches tall] — jester. In a friendly tone with a friendly smile he says, "Come with me. Come with me." And motions with his arms, but he disappears. [I take] two more steps or so and he appears in the tree on the opposite side of the driveway, saying again, "Come with me. Come with me."[18]

A game atmosphere seems to be associated with the little man and he seems open and friendly. Angela makes her way through the thick bushes until at last she reaches the bottom of a long driveway that leads to a large wood house painted white with blue trim.

> The sunlight's shining on its windows and the yard is full of big, beautiful trees. Sitting on the porch is this jester again with his elbow resting on one knee, with the other leg dangling straight down. He's leaning on a pillar and he smiles and motions, and he says, "Come inside, come inside."

The jester suddenly vanishes and the front door groans as it swings open. Angela is now standing in the foyer. She can see the living room, a connecting hallway and kitchen. To her side is a long wooden staircase leading to the second floor.

As she stands there, the front door suddenly closes behind her, a green, grey-white mist begins to swirl about her, "and the feeling is now ominous." In the wall to the right at the bottom of the staircase is a door that suddenly swings opens. In the room:

> The jester is sitting on the windowsill saying in his friendly tone with his friendly smile, "Come inside, come inside." And I do until I'm standing in the middle of the room. Then the door shuts behind me, when all of a sudden [there] appear six

people on the left in black cloaks — I can't see their faces — and six people on the right in white cloaks. They start to move toward me and I'm quite frightened now. And then I hear a strange laugh. And it's the jester on the windowsill. His face becomes all distorted. He throws his head back and laughs in a scary voice. And then I finally awaken.

The events from her first sight of the long driveway to the dreadful laugh of the small man in the pointed hat and green pointed shoes never changed. While she noted the dream in her diary, Angela found the events so frightening that she only discussed it with her best friend. When she was 14 years old, she told her cousin Audrey who believed the dream was a warning, that choices would be put in front of her and that she must tread carefully.

The product of a broken home, Angela had had a difficult upbringing. When she was 16, she began working full time in a long-term care facility in the Fraser Valley. Four years later she was a single mother raising a daughter. Angela remained reluctant to tell anyone about her recurring nightmare. In 1982, though, during a camping trip, she revealed the dream to six friends.

In the summer of that year, Angela became involved with a young man and the couple began looking for a country house for themselves and her daughter, two-year-old Michelle. Angela and Ryan found a vacant farmhouse to rent in the Fraser Valley. The residence had once been part of a large riding stable but the enterprise appeared to have fallen on hard times, and some of the buildings were falling into disrepair.

Although they followed the road to the front entrance of the house, it was possible to see that the yard fell away rather steeply on a terraced slope, and that it was much easier to approach the residence from the back. Simon, the stable caretaker, met them at the back door. He claimed the house had not been empty for very long, but it was full of old furniture, clothing, bottles and other debris that had evidently collected for some time. The walls and windows were filthy and there were rat droppings littering the floors. The rodents had chewed holes through the walls to gain access to shut-up rooms. Despite the deterioration, it was not difficult to see that the house was well built, and it could be "put right" without much difficulty. Simon said he had sprinkled poison throughout the house, and with the caretaker's assurance that the rat problem would soon be over, Angela and Ryan agreed to take the residence.

After Simon left, they inspected the kitchen and were intrigued by a large metal box standing against the wall. Ryan pulled open the latch to reveal the interior of an old-fashioned icebox. Suddenly he ran his left hand down his right arm and shivered. "What was that?" he said. "Did you just touch me?"

"No," Angela said.

"Well, someone touched my arm, I swear it."

For the next two days, Angela, Ryan and several friends used mops, buckets, soaps and detergents to loosen the dirt and grime covering the floors and walls. After some time Kelly, who had been on the camping trip a week earlier when Angela had spoken of her dream, turned to her friend and said, "Let's go out to the front yard to see what work has to be done out there."

From the front door, the two women made their way down the terraced slope as far as a large tree, which seemed about the right size for a child's swing. Suddenly Kelly turned and pointed in the direction from which they had come. "Look," she cried. "Your house, the one in your nightmare."

Angela looked up and stammered, "Oh my God, it is." It was the same large white house with blue trim that had been so vivid during those fitful nights of troubled sleep. Alerted by Kelly, all her friends soon gathered in the yard and were staring up at the clapboard structure.

There was one obvious difference, though, between this building and the house in her nightmare. In her dream, the stairs had been at the side of the porch, but here the steps faced the front. However, it was clear by the nail holes and strips of unpainted wood that the steps had once been at the side of the porch. Angela was certain that she had seen in her dream the residence as it had looked before.

As in her dream, the living room and kitchen were on her left. On her right was the room where the jester and cloaked figures appeared. Even in late summer the room was unusually cold. As they discovered later, none of the electrical outlets seemed to work in this room. This made cleaning all the more difficult, for here their usually reliable vacuum failed to work. Worse for Angela, the same feeling of oppression, which had been so strong in her dream, was present in this room. Up the stairs were three bedrooms: two large bedrooms leading off to the left and right and in the centre a smaller child's room, which would be Michelle's.

Angela, Ryan and their friends spent much of the first night cleaning the house and then slept there. In the morning, the seven people were drinking coffee in the kitchen. Through the window, they could see a little white cottage on the opposite side of the rear driveway. As they sat and talked, someone noticed the front door open and an old lady step out. She was short and stooped, wearing a robe and slippers; in her hair were curlers that were partly covered by a kerchief. At her side were two large dogs, a German shepherd and a Doberman pinscher. As she moved down her walkway she stared at the group of young people in the other house. When she reached her rusty old mailbox, she took out a newspaper. In an effort to be neighbourly, Angela and her friends smiled and waved at the woman, but they received no response. The following morning the woman repeated her walk to the mailbox. While it was clear she was aware of her new neighbours and their friends, she only stared at them coldly.

Several days passed, and although Angela looked for the woman she did not see her again. One day Angela met Simon, the caretaker, and asked him about the person living across the road.

"What are you talking about?" he said. "Nobody's lived in that house for years."

* * * * *

There was something about Angela's new home that seemed to make people uncomfortable. "After I moved in there, the majority of my friends that I would call to come over," Angela remembered, "would get to my driveway or half way up my driveway and then they'd leave." The situation became so serious that few of her friends would come into the house. They were overwhelmed by feelings of foreboding, and Angela had to visit her friends at their homes.

At least as far as the occupants were concerned, there was little doubt that the house was the centre of paranormal activity. Although the "cold room" on the main floor was uncomfortable, she and Ryan believed that the sources of the phenomena were in the basement and attic. The entrance to the unused attic was boarded off, and no one summoned the courage to pull the boards free and examine that area of the house. The basement had a thick, unpleasant, earthy odour, and neither Ryan nor Angela ever stayed there long.

Nowhere in the house did Angela and Ryan really feel comfortable. The couple always had the disconcerting feeling that they were under the eye of someone or something unseen. This was particularly true while they were showering. One night they were awakened by the sound of breaking glass coming from downstairs. When Ryan went down to investigate he found a picture that had been hanging on the wall shattered on the floor.

On another occasion, Angela and Ryan were lying in bed late one night when they heard footsteps and voices on the stairs. By the time their visitors neared the top step, their voices were almost clear enough for their words to be understood. Ryan sat up in bed and challenged them. Immediately the noise stopped, but there was no sound of footsteps retreating down the stairs. Another night the couple were in bed when the lights and appliances suddenly went on. The incident was short-lived, lasting no more than 30 seconds.

A few months after moving in, Angela and Ryan took in Greg, a weekend boarder who spent the week away at a logging camp. He was given the third bedroom upstairs. One night toward the end of the week, Angela and Ryan were lying in bed in the dark but still awake when they heard their bedroom door open. Wondering if their boarder had come home early, they shouted, "Is that you, Greg?" In the darkened room, there was no reply. "But the body," Angela recalled, "moved closer to the bedside and we could feel it breathing." They offered a prayer and the entity seemed to leave. When they finally were able to turn on the light, the door was closed tight.

Ryan and Angela had the impression that the ghost of a 17-year-old girl haunted the house, and that she was the same entity that had touched Ryan's arm when the couple were preparing to move in. She wanted something from Ryan, and Angela felt threatened by the presence. "I even had a twisted sort of jealous feeling, it was really odd. And she was standing beside my bedside, almost like she just wanted rid of me."

Not all of the bizarre events occurred in the house. One day, Simon happened to mention that a horse show was to be held on Sunday at the stables and that the family could go if they wished. Angela, who had taken riding lessons before, wanted to attend. On that day Angela, Ryan, Michelle and Ryan's friend, Jack, walked from the barn to the stables where the show was to be held and joined the spectators. After it was over they went home and Angela and Ryan returned to their daily routine. The horse show probably would have been forgotten had it not been that one of Angela's cats was missing. After searching around the house, she visited the neighbours to ask whether anyone had seen her pet. During one stop, Angela asked the couple if they had enjoyed the horse show.

"What horse show?" they said. There was no such event and if one had been planned they certainly would have been involved. At another house farther up the road, Angela received the same response.

It was then that Angela recalled something odd about the crowd at the horse show: the clothes people wore seemed a decade or more out of fashion. She had been interested in the events and had spent little time looking at the crowd. Angela wondered whether she, Ryan, Jack and Michelle "had attended something that never happened."

* * * * *

As the weeks passed, petty arguments between Angela and Ryan became more acrimonious, and eventually the couple agreed that Ryan should move out. Angela remained and was able to pay the rent by taking in several boarders. Eventually, though, the oppressive atmosphere seemed to weigh upon her.

Angela began going to college and discussed the strange occurrences in her psychology class. In the spring of 1982, when she mentioned she had decided to leave the area, one young female student expressed interest in renting the house to study and write about it. Angela introduced her to the owner of the house before packing up the car and locating to another area of the province. Although the young woman had struck Angela as a stable person, she later discovered that "within three months of moving in she committed suicide."

In 1985 Angela returned to the Fraser Valley to attend a wedding and drove with a male friend to her former residence. They climbed the steps to the rear of the house: "When we got to the back door, it was open. We heard this typewriter from inside the house. We knocked and the typewriter stopped. But no one would come to the door."

After enduring the silence for several minutes her friend said, "We're out of here, let's go." They returned to the car and drove away.

* * * * *

One of the oddest aspects of this strange and complex story is the elderly woman with the two dogs who appeared to occupy the little house across the driveway. While she never saw the jester in her sleep after moving into the house, one night Angela dreamed that the woman was coming toward her. Frightened, she woke up in a panic. Only later did she conclude that the person might have been her grandmother. It seems plausible to Angela that the apparition of the woman with the two guard dogs could have been a warning to be aware of the dangers she would be facing. While such occurrences are usually very personal, and limited to the individual involved, this was not the case here. Seven people saw the old woman and her dogs on two occasions.

Although the incidents took place more than 20 years ago, Angela clearly recalls that difficult period of her life. It seemed that the malevolent forces that occupied the old house were able to twist time.

THE RAPPING GHOST

Ghosts usually confine themselves to one house at a time, but on the odd occasion they have been known to haunt more than one location. This is the case in the small community of Wells, not far from Barkerville. Unlike Barkerville, Wells is comparatively new, owing its existence to a rich gold strike there in 1932.

In Wells there is a house owned by Ron Candy. On the surface there is nothing particularly unusual about the house: like most of the others on the same block, it was built some time in the early 1930s. During the 12 years Candy lived in the house, he experienced a number of odd incidents. The most common phenomenon involved rapping — usually three definite knocks — on the roof or back wall of his house. The sound is quite distinct: on one occasion a guest staying in the house woke Candy in the middle of the night, convinced that someone was trying to break in.

There were other unusual occurrences as well. In winter, particularly, perfume has been frequently noted just outside Candy's house. Those experiencing the scent have said that it occurs only in a clearly defined location. "You'd be walking along," Ron Candy recalled, "and you'd walk into this column of very pungent perfume. You could walk in and out of it ... and you wouldn't smell it anywhere else."[19] It is unlikely that the perfume could have been carried on the wind from some other location: the column containing the scent was no more than a foot across.

Candy's residence has not been the only focus of these weird episodes: a number have taken place at a neighbouring dwelling, a log house occupied until recently by the Keeley family (not their real name). Although Candy's nearest neighbours were the Keeleys, their house was built on the opposite side of a cul-de-sac. During the time they lived in the cabin the Keeleys also heard rapping noises, apparently coming from the roof, and the ghost of a woman was apparently witnessed by at least one family member. The Keeleys have subsequently moved away from the log house and new occupants have moved in, but the mysterious rapping sound still continues. (The spectre, however, has not been seen again.) The Keeley house, although of quite recent construction, was built on the foundation of an old cabin that apparently predated the town of Wells, but unfortunately nothing more is known about the old cabin or its former occupants.

* * * * *

It is interesting to note that in two of the houses discussed in this chapter, considerable repairs were being undertaken. Some psychical investigators have postulated that physical changes to a dwelling bring about paranormal occurrences. One classic case comes from England. When a fire escape was added to a Northamptonshire inn quite recently, the resident ghost, said to be Queen Mary of Scotland, appeared to three different occupants of the "haunted room" on three successive nights.

Other strange events have been reported not far from London, England, where half a wall, the wainscotting for example, along the lower half of a hallway, has been removed. The resident ghost has reappeared sure enough, but the lower half of him — the half opposite the new wall — is missing.

Haunted Places

THE GHOSTS OF BEACON HILL PARK

On warm, sunny summer days, the beautiful flower gardens of Victoria's Beacon Hill Park offer a pleasant diversion from the noise and bustle of the city. A short drive from the downtown core takes a person to a pleasant, restful 154-acre site. Yet at night Beacon Hill Park can be a sinister place.

Even before the coming of Europeans, the island people who lived in the two communities near the area were subject to disease, which killed many villagers. The southeast slope of the park is the location of many burial cairns. In 1986, park staff inadvertently dug up and removed the stone grave markers, which upset the Native peoples. Some ghost researchers have speculated that this act has disturbed the dead and that after sunset, the spirits search for their cairns.

There are other ghosts as well. Since the mid-1970s the apparition of a tall, young, slender, tanned blond woman wearing white pants has been seen at sunrise on the rocky prominence near Douglas and Superior streets. What witnesses found particularly frightening was that the woman was obviously terror stricken, with a muted scream on her lips and her arms held up to ward off an attacker.

Although Beacon Hill Park is pleasant in the daylight, some eerie entities have been seen after dark. (COURTESY OF D. M. BELYK)

The identity of the apparition was not determined until some time later, when on the afternoon of November 3, 1983, a park employee stumbled on a badly decomposed body. The remains had been placed in a shallow grave and were partially exposed by the fall rains. The body was that of a 21-year-old woman who had been reported missing by her husband more than four months earlier.

Surprisingly, as Skelton and Kozocari noted in their collection of ghost stories, the woman was certainly alive during the time the apparition was first sighted.[1] A further twist to this haunt is that the victim had long dark hair and pale skin, and was wearing blue jeans, while the apparition was seen as if it were a photographic negative of the living person.

After the young woman's death, the ghost continued to make an appearance at sunrise near the park's Southgate entrance. Now seen as a positive image with long, dark hair thrown back, her head looks up, the silent scream still on her lips, a shocking reminder of the savagery of her death.

* * * * *

Another unusual ghost apparently haunts the park. The discovery of the body of a 40-year-old homeless person in the spring of 1984 did not create much excitement in the city's media. The man was believed to have drowned accidentally in the duck pond.

The incident would have been entirely forgotten if it had not been for Janet Holmes and her husband Brian (not their real names) who were walking through the park about five years after the unfortunate man's death. It was about eleven o'clock at night when they saw someone leaning against a tall tree. As they approached Janet noted a particularly ancient pair of leather shoes. What was amazing, though, was that the torso and head were missing. Nothing could be seen above the legs. Bravely, Janet and her husband circled the tree for a better look, but from any angle they could see only half a ghost. Perplexed, the couple walked away.

Was the body that of the homeless person? The decrepit shoes would certainly point to a destitute person. However, why did only half of the body appear to the couple? Like the murdered woman, the reasons for particular forms of ghostly appearances are often a mystery.

THE OLD LADY'S BED

Of all household furnishings, the bed is probably the most personal, because it is such an integral part of the life process. Until a century ago, it was frequently the place of an individual's first and last breath. It is now common for people to enter and exit life via places less personal, but one's own bed remains the most important single piece of furniture. People usually spend at least one-quarter of their time beneath the covers.

Even after death, it seems that some ghosts do not wish to give up this connection to the material world. Indeed, this is what

Dave and Joyce Watson discovered after purchasing a secondhand bed for their young daughter.

* * * * *

In early 1980, Dave and Joyce Watson were expecting the birth of their second child, and it was clear that two-year-old Lisa would have to give up her crib for the new baby. Joyce's mother lived in a retirement home in Burnaby, one of whose residents had recently died. The late tenant's relatives were selling her possessions and Dave and Joyce decided to purchase the bed, a single unit made up of a metal frame, box spring, mattress and a mustard-coloured velour headboard. Though the unit was quite ugly, it was at least practical.

Not long after the birth of their son, Brent, the Watsons moved into a new house in Port Coquitlam. With them was their dog, a young German shepherd cross named Shep, who was very loyal and protective toward all family members.

In the new house, Lisa was given her own room with the secondhand bed. Joyce soon observed that although before moving to their new home, Lisa had always fallen asleep quickly at bedtime, now the opposite was true. "She would always cry," Joyce recalled, "and it wasn't one of those cries like 'I don't want to go to sleep.' It was gasping and sobbing."[2]

Dave and Joyce had noted something strange about Lisa's bedroom: it seemed to be unusually cold. It was built over the open carport, but so was Brent's room, and in contrast, the nursery was warm.

There was no nightlight in Lisa's room. Instead, Joyce turned on a radio at low volume to provide a comforting background noise. One early October night, about three months after they had moved in, Dave and Joyce put the two children to bed and went downstairs to the family room to watch television. Dave lit the fireplace as the couple relaxed on the couch. From upstairs, the Watsons heard the cries of their daughter. As was often the case, Lisa wouldn't settle. When Dave went up to see if he could calm her, the little girl told her father a bizarre story. Once the light is turned off and the door is shut, Lisa said, an old lady comes and shakes the bed.

When Joyce heard her husband's story, she was sceptical. "Come on, Dave," she said. "Lisa isn't three yet. Where can she get a story like that? She only watches 'Sesame Street.' "

"That's what she told me," Dave replied emphatically.

Joyce went upstairs to her daughter's bedroom where the child was crying. "Would you feel better if Shep stayed in the room with you?" her mother asked.

"Yes," sobbed Lisa.

In a few minutes Shep was brought to Lisa's room where he remained after the light was turned off and the door was closed. Even with the dog's company, though, Lisa continued to cry. After a few minutes, Joyce climbed the stairs again.

When she turned the handle and pushed the door open, there was a sudden commotion in the room. "Shep," Joyce recalled, "shot between my legs and ran down [the stairs to the basement and] into the family room. I followed him and when I got into the family room there was Dave sitting on the sofa in front of the fire with the dog cowering under his legs."

After Shep's reaction that night, Joyce considered that there might indeed be something to her daughter's story. Was it true that a ghost was haunting Lisa's bedroom? Dave discussed the matter with a work mate who was psychic. The man visited the Watsons and spent a few minutes alone in the bedroom. When he came out he explained that he had felt "something" but he was not sure what it was.

Another friend, who was also psychic, was more certain where the hostile energy arose: the bed's original owner. "Get rid of the bed," she said. "That old lady doesn't want to harm Lisa, but she doesn't want her in the bed. That's why she's shaking the mattress."

The Watsons disposed of the old bed, and got their daughter a new frame, box spring, mattress and headboard. From her first night in her new bed, Lisa had no difficulty sleeping. The old woman who shook her mattress was gone. The room, too, was more comfortable. "That icy chill," Joyce recalled, "believe me, it disappeared."

THE PHANTOM OF THE BURN UNIT

During the time of the Burn Unit haunting, the Vancouver General Hospital (VGH) ordered its staff not to discuss the strange incidents with anyone outside the hospital. Hospital authorities quite rightly feared that publicity would disrupt the functioning of the unit. The public is fascinated by buildings supposedly inhabited by ghosts, and one can imagine crowds of ghost seekers interrupting the vital work of the nurses and doctors.

However, now that the building which housed the old Burn Unit has been demolished, and a new, ghost-free facility has been opened in its place, hospital authorities have allowed the nurses to speak out. It has been years since the episodes involving the young patient began, and most of the staff there at the time have moved on to other hospitals; still, there are nurses working there who recall the events which occurred after the tragic death of one burn victim.

* * * * *

Nursing is a very demanding profession. Even in the midst of crisis the nurse is expected to carry on coolly and efficiently. From their first days in training, student nurses are taught observational skills: to see, hear, feel and touch. Thus, when the incidents began in the VGH Burn Unit in early 1976, they were witnessed by thoroughly professional observers. There was no question in the minds of many of the nurses working there that the Burn Unit was haunted.

People who work in large grain-storage facilities are aware that grain dust is a highly explosive substance. Over the years there have been many grain elevator explosions in other parts of the continent, but workers at Burrard Terminals Ltd. in North Vancouver felt they were less at risk than their prairie counterparts. The damp British Columbia climate, it was believed, moistened the grain and made it less volatile. The fallacy of this idea was tragically demonstrated on October 3, 1975, when a small fire in a conveyor belt touched off a massive explosion that killed one man instantly and sent 16 others to hospital. Those suffering serious burns were sent to the Burn Unit.

One of the victims in critical condition was 28-year-old Douglas Woods (not his real name). As nurses and doctors examined the young man it was clear that the prognosis was not good. Victims of severe burns often cling to life for a few days, weeks or even months before finally succumbing to their injuries, suffering terrible pain before eventually being released by death.

As the staff working in the intensive care area soon discovered, Douglas was no ordinary patient: he had an incredible will to live. Even though he faced tremendous pain, he fought on. Aided by a warm family and close friends, he continued to beat the odds, yet, slowly, the pain of his ordeal sapped the young man's strength.

Just before his death, Douglas confided that he was sure he was going to die. "I'm very tired," he told a nurse, "and I've had so much pain."[3] The nurse who was with him was surprised because in the three months he'd been on the ward he'd come so far. She tried to give him some encouragement, but he seemed quite resigned to his fate. The next night his heart suddenly stopped.

Unit staff found it difficult to accept Douglas's sudden passing. His tenacity in the face of incredible pain had been inspiring. However, the young man made it plain that he was not really very far away. Soon after his death, a relief night nurse from another ward went into 415, Douglas's old room. She looked in the direction of what had been his bed to see the covers suddenly shift, just as if someone had rolled over. There was also a noise coming from that direction, the soft, rhythmical sound of breathing, but nobody had been admitted to Douglas's bed.

Not long after the first incident, there were others. One of the other nurses reported entering 415, which was unoccupied, and being unable to shake a very powerful feeling that someone was in the room with her. The two-bed room was used for intensive-care patients and between the beds there was a sink. The nurse's eyes moved around until her gaze reached the area between the beds. In front of the sink she watched a vague shape move slowly around the end of the bed and out through the door.

On another occasion, a male nurse, Denny Conrad, and another nurse were quickly readying the room for a new admission. Conrad was preoccupied with preparations so as he came into the room with a load of laundry bags, he was barely aware of his colleague's white form standing with a dressings tray. As he turned to speak to the other person in the room, the dressings fell to the floor. "It wasn't her at all," Conrad said. "It was [Douglas]."[4] Conrad abruptly turned and left the room. In retrospect it seems clear that Douglas was only trying to help prepare the dressing for the patient, but nurses, like almost everyone else, have difficulty dealing with ghosts, and Conrad was severely shaken by the incident.

It was not only staff members who saw Douglas. A nurse reported an incident involving a woman who was admitted with terrible burns. It was obvious that she had only a short time to live and all the staff could do was to make her as comfortable as possible. As a new shift came on the nurse entered the room to check on the patient. The patient looked up and said, "Oh, by the way, there was a strange young man just in here visiting me."

The nurse was shocked that anyone outside the woman's immediate family could have visited this critically ill patient.

"Who did you say was here?" she asked.

"He said his name was [Douglas]," came the patient's reply.[5]

On another occasion, nurse Alice Bishop (not her real name) recalled making rounds with other ward staff one morning. A man who had been badly burned was in room 413, next to Douglas's former room. She spoke with the patient for a moment before he suddenly said, "I'd like to thank that young doctor who took the time last night to come in and help me with the pain."[6]

All the staff in the room were surprised, but no one said anything until they were outside the patient's door. They questioned each other about who the patient could possibly mean; there should have been no doctor on the ward the previous evening. Finally a nurse phoned the night shift staff, now off duty, and confirmed that indeed no doctor had visited the ward. Much perplexed, one staff member went back into the patient's room and asked him to recall the person who had been in to see him last night. The description fit only one person: it was Douglas.

"The nurses on the floor," Ms. Bishop later acknowledged, "never told the patient that the young man who had been so helpful was a ghost."

Douglas seemed to have two missions on the ward. The first was to ease the suffering of other patients. This was not surprising to the staff; after all, he had suffered considerable pain for a long time, and it seemed only logical, knowing Douglas, that he would try to make the pain easier for other burn victims. Douglas's second mission, it seems, was to announce to the staff that he was still very definitely in the Burn Unit. It was the way Douglas chose to announce this fact that caused so much difficulty with the nurses.

As Conrad recalled, "Other night shifts that I worked there — especially night shifts — you'd be walking by and the radio would be full blast all of a sudden. The toilet would flush, or you'd be sitting at the nursing station and the [call] light for 415 would go on." Of course, the room would be unoccupied at the time.[7]

Ms. Bishop related an incident concerning a nurse who had gone into Douglas's former room to hang a bottle of intravenous solution. "Suddenly she felt strange, and then very cold, like she was covered in ice. Displaying remarkable courage she said in an even voice, 'Look [Douglas], I know you're here, but I'm really busy tonight, so please don't interrupt me.' Then suddenly the coldness lifted and she was able to go on about her work."[8]

For a time the strange occurrences were so common that most of the staff simply tried to adjust to the situation. Room 415 was the centre of the paranormal activity and nurses frequently would take only ten-minute shifts in that room. The intense cold, the strange prickly feeling in the scalp, taps turning, toilets flushing and lights going on and off — it was too much for them. They couldn't take it for long. As Conrad recalled later, "I'd walk in there and [my] hair would stand right up. And you knew he was there. It was just awful."[9]

However, although the haunting put the staff under considerable tension, there was never any feeling of evil. The staff were convinced that Douglas simply wanted to make sure everyone knew he was not far away. As time passed, the disturbances decreased, yet it was only when the staff moved to a new facility and the old building was torn down that the haunting stopped completely.

If there is a lesson to be drawn from the Burn Unit haunting it is that ghosts cannot exist on the same plane with living human beings, at least not without causing considerable difficulty. Douglas was a warm and caring person who wished only to relieve the suffering of others who, like himself, faced acute distress, but his presence made it very difficult for the Burn Unit to operate properly. It is not Douglas's fault, of course. People find it hard to overcome their fear of ghosts, even when, like Douglas, the ghosts have the best of intentions.

MORE ON DOUGLAS

"All of a sudden I had this absolutely horrendous vision of this face … this incredibly terrified screaming face just rushing at me,"[10] Rosemary Leavitt recalled. Although she wasn't aware of it at the time, her vision was connected with the explosion at Burrard Terminals on October 3, 1975. She had a friend, Douglas Woods, who was working there.

Rosemary had met Douglas through a mutual acquaintance, and soon the two became involved. Although their romance was short lived — they did not have the same interests — Rosemary and Douglas parted friends and kept in touch.

In the autumn of 1975, Rosemary went with her mother to Williams Lake for a brief holiday. They took a room at a hotel and planned to visit relatives in the area. Each morning, while her mother went to the café for coffee, Rosemary spent about 30 minutes in her room meditating. The young woman had recently completed a course with a difficult final exam and she was still suffering the after-effects of test anxiety. Friends had told Rosemary that meditation would help put the experience behind her. As she recalled, though, this session was not what she had anticipated: the image of the screaming man seemed to come out of nowhere. Rosemary did not recognize the person or the location of the event, but it was frightening and she was deeply shaken.

That evening, Rosemary and her mother went to dinner at the home of her cousin, Noreen. As the meal was prepared, the news was on television, and the lead item was the fire at Burrard Terminals in North Vancouver.

"That's [Douglas]," Rosemary blurted out. "That's where he works." She watched as the television showed the ambulances unloading the victims on gurneys at the hospital. She knew without doubt that one of the badly burned bodies belonged to Douglas.

Because of the danger of infection, Douglas's friends were not allowed in his room. Most of the burns were to his arms and lower body and his face was almost untouched. From his appearance, it was difficult for his friends to realize how severely he had been injured. Douglas, for his part, would put on a brave act, and even under the pain, he kept his sense of humour. When Rosemary arrived at the hospital, he would sometimes be sitting up in bed. "He'd wink at me and blow me a kiss," Rosemary recalled, "like 'here's another one of my fans'."

As the months passed, he remained isolated. Rosemary and Sandy, his girlfriend, and other friends continued to visit though they could see him only by looking through the glass in the door to his room.

One winter day, Rosemary planned to visit the hospital, but she was an inexperienced driver and a few flakes of snow had begun to fall. There was a window alcove in her Vancouver apartment where she had placed pillows so she curled up there and watched as the grey winter sky faded into the murky gloom of night. The glow from the streetlights seemed to illuminate each snowflake as it fell, and it was not long before Rosemary was slipping off to sleep.

Then Douglas was suddenly before her. "He was dancing, literally hopping from one foot to the other saying, 'Look at me. Look at me. I'm whole!' He was just so happy." Abruptly his manner changed. He stepped back from her and said, "You're not good for me. I can't be around here."

Rosemary's last recollection of Douglas was that a tall, slender, fair nurse approached him and said, "Come [Douglas]."

"He turned around and walked away with her."

A few hours later, Rosemary received word of Douglas's death.

* * * * *

While it is not difficult to ascribe any number of meanings to Douglas's words — after all, he was severing his connection with at least part of the material plane — Rosemary was left with feelings of guilt, fearing that somehow she had failed her friend.

THE OLD CRAIGFLOWER SCHOOL

There are a number of frightening stories relating to the old Craigflower School building in Saanich on Vancouver Island. The origin of the following tale is not known, so its authenticity must be suspect. It has been suggested that a summary of this particular incident may have been given by the long-time school caretaker, Hugh Palliser, to the archives in Victoria, but if so there is no record of it, today.

* * * * *

The first Craigflower School was completed in 1855 by Vancouver Island's colonial administration for the children of Hudson's Bay Company employees and other settlers who had established farms in the area. The school was on Victoria's Portage Inlet in a spot that was conveniently reached by boat and horse, but because many farms were isolated it was necessary for some of the students to board in. Living quarters for the teacher and students were thus included in the school plan.

Craigflower School was a tribute to the increasing self reliance of the early settlers; wood for construction came from the HBC's own steam-powered sawmill on Craigflower Farm, not far from the school, and the bricks used for the foundation were manufactured in a local kiln.

The wreck of the 150-ton ship, *Major Tompkins*, in 1855 provided Craigflower with one important school fixture. While the ship was eventually battered to pieces on the rocks off Esquimalt, all the passengers and crew escaped with their lives; there was even time to save the ship's bell which was duly presented to the school. From then on, the *Major Tompkins'* bell dutifully called students to class at Craigflower.

The old school served until 1911, when a new structure was completed nearby. After the new facility was complete, the living quarters in the old school were retained as a residence for the school's caretaker. It was when caretaker Hugh Palliser and his family were occupying the residence that the haunting occurred.

One day in early September 1918, the rotting old Craigflower bridge collapsed, taking with it a big gravel truck. While the driver escaped unhurt, the truck was partially submerged in about ten feet of water. The old bridge adjoined the Craigflower School grounds; thus, when operations to salvage the truck began, it was necessary to attach a heavy anchor line to school property so that the truck could be winched up the gorge.

Palliser stood in the school yard watching the operation. The job went well enough until workmen began clearing away brush and debris from the site selected for anchoring the winch line. One of the men gave a yell as his shovel turned something over. It wasn't much, just a few small bones. Thinking that it

Craigflower School. (THE HERITAGE GROUP COLLECTION)

was only the remains of some small animal the man went back to work.

It wasn't long, however, before he again stopped suddenly. This time the blade of his shovel had turned over something that was quite unmistakable. Clearly exposed in the hole were a number of long, thin bones. The caretaker could easily identify them as the bones of a human arm. The man dug carefully now, and soon a human skull was exposed. Palliser took it from the shallow excavation and began brushing off the heavy clay soil that clung to it. It was yellowed with age, and many of the teeth were missing. Digging further in the hole the man found a complete human skeleton. Like the skull, all the bones were very brown and old-looking.

Hugh Palliser walked back to the school, returning a few minutes later with a large wooden box. The caretaker and the workmen gathered the bones and placed them in the box. As far as the caretaker was concerned, it was obvious what had happened: the workmen had accidentally disturbed the ancient grave of an Indian.

"My youngest daughter is studying anatomy," he told the workmen. "We'll let her have a look at these and put them [together]."[11] When they had recovered everything Palliser closed the lid tightly. The men returned to the task of anchoring the support cable while Palliser picked up the box and carried it to the woodshed which adjoined the old school building. He put the box on one of the long shelves which lined the walls of the shed and then returned to his own tasks around the school.

After supper that evening, Palliser and his wife settled around the kitchen stove to read. It was unusually cold for early September, but the schoolhouse was quite comfortable. Then the quiet of the evening was suddenly broken by a sharp click. It was the sound made by the latch being raised on the door leading from the kitchen to the woodshed. Both put down their books and waited for someone to come in through the kitchen door. The door was a crude affair consisting of five or six boards laid edge to edge and several crosspieces, held shut by means of an ordinary thumb latch. The mechanism was quite simple, but once the latch was shut it could not be lifted without applying considerable pressure. As the Pallisers watched, the door swung open, but nothing came in except a cold blast of air.

Palliser got up and walked through the woodshed to the outside door, but to his surprise it was closed tightly. "Funny," he said to himself. "I'd have sworn the outside door was open by the way the wind came in." Returning to the kitchen, he securely closed the door to the woodshed.

The family passed the remainder of the evening quietly. As they were preparing for bed, however, the caretaker again heard the distinctive click of the door latch being opened. He returned to the kitchen to investigate. Once more as he watched, the door to the shed swung open. Again a blast of cold air poured out from the inky blackness of the shed. Palliser took a lantern and returned to the woodshed, but the outside door was still bolted shut. The cold wind seemed to arise out of nowhere.

In the lantern light he examined the woodshed. There was no hole in the roof of the shed. There was no gap along the outside walls. No space had suddenly opened up to let the elements in. Wood for the stove was stacked neatly in a pile on the floor, while on the walls his tools were properly hung in place. Along one wall, his wife's preserves filled the shelves, and along another were household odds and ends the family had stored. Nothing was out of order.

Palliser was just about to return to the kitchen when the light from the lantern fell on the wooden box he had placed there earlier in the day. He pulled the lid off the box. There in the pale light the caretaker could see the ancient yellow skull grinning up at him. As he looked on, the lantern light flickered wildly, making the shadows dance. It was as if the bones had come to life. He quickly returned the lid to the box and left.

In the kitchen, he again securely fastened the door to the woodshed before retiring. There was no further disturbance that night, but the following evening Palliser was ready for whoever or, as he feared, whatever, was behind the door to the woodshed. After his wife and children had retired early to bed, the caretaker sat alone in the kitchen reading the paper and waiting. His chair was placed only inches from the door, and on the floor next to him was a lantern.

It was quite late when he heard the noise again: the unmistakable click of the latch. Immediately Palliser looked up, and as he watched dumbfounded the latch slowly lifted and stopped in the up position. Quickly grabbing his lantern, he closed his hand on the latch handle, then flung the door open.

Palliser was a down-to-earth Yorkshireman, certainly not the kind of individual to give way to wild flights of fancy. He had often heard the wind whistle through the old schoolhouse on lonely winter nights, and knew it for what it was. He also knew that what he had seen and heard these last two nights was no figment of his imagination and that when the lantern light filled the black space behind the door, he would be staring at whatever had moved the mechanism of the latch. The flickering light played across the woodshed to reveal nothing but that same icy blast of wind. Palliser walked through the woodshed to the outside door. It was just as he left it earlier that evening: bolted shut from the inside. No living being could have got in there.

Next he took the box from the shelf and opened it. There in the dim light, the skull looked up at him; now though, the grin seemed evil. The caretaker knew what he had to do. He took a spade from among the tools in the shed, and opened the outside door. With his lantern in one hand, and his spade and the box of bones under his arm, Palliser walked out into the pitch-black night.

Somewhere in the school yard Palliser dug a new grave for the yellowed bones. When the hole was deep enough he placed the box in the grave. Even years later, he never revealed exactly where the ancient bones were buried, but his assumption had been correct: with the last spadeful of earth spread over the yellowed bones, this particular haunting of the old Craigflower School came abruptly to an end.

*　*　*　*　*

The Craigflower schoolhouse is the oldest school building still surviving in western Canada, and is operated as a heritage museum by the provincial government. The old school has been the site of many strange goings-on, and those associated with the museum over the years have reported many unusual happenings.

C. J. (Jerry) Clark will not forget the period between 1970 and 1980 when he acted as live-in caretaker at the Craigflower School museum. One night Clark was sitting at a table in the school answering some letters, with his dog, Dixie, lying on the floor beside him. Suddenly the dog began to growl. Clark put his pen down and listened closely. There were voices coming from the other side of the wall in the area of the washroom. Clark checked the room but could find nothing to account for the sounds. He then expanded his search to include the entire building, but there was no sign of intruders either inside or outside the building. "There was no sign of anybody around anywhere."[12]

There were other occasions when unexplained noises were heard. Once, just after the last visitor had left, Clark and his wife, who had been acting as tour guides, stopped outside for a break. Suddenly there was a tremendous banging and clatter somewhere in the school. When the Clarks arrived to investigate, the noise stopped abruptly. Again, there were no intruders to be found anywhere on Craigflower School property.

At other times the school bell from the old *Major Tompkins* would suddenly start ringing on its own. Then, adding to the cacophony, other school bells would join in until the building shook with the sound. "We thought it was vandals — kids running around — but there was not a thing," Clark recalled. "What started the bells to suddenly ring always was a mystery."

On one occasion Clark heard what sounded like someone dragging a chain down a set of stairs which led to the top floor. Again the caretaker could see nothing that would explain these noises.

What could account for the Craigflower School phenomena? One explanation may be that a number of ancient remains had been disturbed there. Apparently the Craigflower School property included part of a large Indian burial ground. An article in the Victoria *Daily Times* for December 20, 1911, noted that while contractors were excavating the construction of the new Craigflower

School (across the street from the old one), they came across five skulls buried with a number of arrow heads. It is conceivable that there are yet other restless spirits in the vicinity of the old school.

THE PHANTOM OF THE LINKS

She has been given many names over the years — the Watcher, the April Ghost, the Oak Bay Ghost, or the Ghost of Golf Course Point. After a quiet period in the 1970s when there were few sightings, Victoria's most sought-after ghost has again become active. On moon-lit spring nights, local high school and university students continue to make an annual pilgrimage to the Victoria Golf Club where they hope to see the elusive spectre for themselves. It is not surprising that this beautiful lady in the diaphanous wedding dress has such a special appeal to young people, for as legend has it she is, literally, their ghost. According to local folk tales, this particular apparition is seen only by young couples, but there's a catch: this is not a spot to take your true love, for the tale also says that couples seeing the ghost will never marry.

Actually, there is little romance associated with the story of Doris Gravlin, the young woman who is thought to haunt the Victoria Golf Course; her death was simply a senseless waste. The young and attractive auburn-haired nurse was liked by almost everyone, but in September 1936, she was having difficulty with her estranged husband, Victor. Victor was sports editor at one of Victoria's daily newspapers, and he had developed a severe drinking problem. In the late summer of 1936, Doris had been separated from him for almost two years.

After leaving her husband, Mrs. Gravlin was hired as a private nurse by Mrs. Kathleen Richardson, who lived in an apartment on Beach Drive in Oak Bay. Mrs. Richardson later testified before an inquest that Mrs. Gravlin left about eight o'clock on the evening of September 22, to go for a walk. She never returned.

Five days later a Victoria Golf Club caddy, John Johnson, was looking for a lost ball on the shoreline near the seventh tee, when he

The Victoria Golf Course. (PHOTOGRAPH BY THE AUTHOR)

noticed a woman's sweater lying on the beach. As he bent to pick it up he saw Mrs. Gravlin's body in a patch of tall grass and bush.

The subsequent police investigation determined that the woman had been murdered in a patch of wild broom beside the seventh hole and her body dragged down to the beach. An autopsy revealed that she had been beaten and then strangled, probably by a piece of cord which was then used to drag the body to the beach. Strangely, the woman's white kid leather shoes, which she had been known to be wearing the night of her death, were missing and could not be found, even after a careful search of the vicinity of the murder.

The investigation soon turned up one interesting fact: Doris Gravlin's estranged husband, Victor, also disappeared the night of September 22. Gravlin, who had been living with his parents, told them about eight o'clock that evening that he was going out for a stroll. He never returned. After the inquest, the police issued a warrant for his arrest in connection with the murder of his wife.

Despite the best efforts of police, however, Gravlin could not be located. On October 25, exactly four weeks after the discovery of the remains of Mrs. Gravlin, her husband's body was found; a man rowing off the shore of the golf links saw it entangled in a bed of kelp. It was estimated he had been dead four weeks. In the inside pocket of his coat police found Mrs. Gravlin's missing shoes.

At that time the full story was never printed in the paper, but people who knew the couple were able to put a human face on the tragedy, and since many of them were employed by Victoria newspapers, the story slowly leaked into print. The picture that emerged was of two young people who were desperately in love. There was only one problem, but it was enough to drive them apart — liquor turned Victor Gravlin from a typical "nice guy" into a monster. It wasn't that Victor didn't sincerely try to give up alcohol; in fact he attempted to quit repeatedly, but always without success. Even faced with the end of his marriage he could not stop.

It was said that on the day of the tragedy Victor phoned Doris and promised to give up whisky. She agreed to meet him that evening at one of their favourite spots — the Oak Bay Beach Hotel, not far from the Victoria Golf Course — so that they could talk about a possible reconciliation. After having tea at the hotel restaurant, the couple went for a walk on the golf course. At about nine o'clock that evening someone living not far from the golf course heard a terrible scream. Since Victor was not seen after his wife's death, it is believed that he drowned himself soon after he killed her.

With the discovery of Victor's body the police closed the official investigation into the murder of Doris Gravlin, but the unfortunate young woman was not about to be forgotten. Exactly when strange occurrences began in the area of Golf Course Point, is not known, but by the 1940s there were already tales of eerie happenings there after dark.

An early report concerns an unnamed fisherman. One evening at dusk the man was casting a line from a rocky outcropping which jutted away from the shore beside the golf course. Later he couldn't say what drew his attention, but when he glanced toward the shore, he saw a young woman standing at the edge of the water, on the lee side of the point. She was quite close to him, no more than a couple of yards away, and he could see her quite clearly, even though the light was beginning to fail. She appeared real, but what struck him as odd was that she was wearing an old-fashioned brown suit (not the wedding dress which was to become identified with her later). Also, he noticed she wore a morose expression, and just stood there staring sadly out to sea.

He made a couple of casts while the young woman continued to stand there silently. "Then," he was later reported to have said, "she suddenly hurried down as if she was going to meet someone, and on the way, she vanished. I saw her kind of melt away."[13]

In early April 1964, there was an incident involving a 16-year-old boy, Anthony Gregson, and his girlfriend (the girl asked not to be identified, although she corroborated the boy's story). About nine o'clock on that pleasant spring evening, Gregson and the girl were walking on the golf course near the small point of land that juts out into the bay. Both youngsters were familiar with the folk tales of the ghost, and they laughed and joked lightheartedly about the spectre. At first the young couple was not aware of anything unusual, but as Gregson later told reporters, inexplicably the atmosphere seemed to change. There was suddenly something very strange in the air, and they both became unusually serious. Then they saw a ghost.

Gregson was obviously shocked by the incident — he later described the apparition as an incredible thousand yards away — but he had no doubt about what he saw. He took the phantom to be a woman because it was wearing a dress. However, unlike the apparition seen by the fisherman, there was no chance this one could be mistaken for a living person. It was a sort of luminous grey in colour, and it was surrounded by an aura. "The ghost," according to young Gregson, "moved with much more ease than a human and a certain grace of action, especially in her arms. Other features were less distinct."[14]

She moved along the beach, but what he noticed as particularly strange was that her feet seemed to pass over the pebbles on the shore without coming into contact with them. As the couple watched, the ghostly shape continued along the edge of the water. When she finally reached the end of the point she stopped abruptly and gazed out over the water as if waiting for someone. "I would rather like to think she was," Gregson added.

When the couple finally turned to leave, the ghost was still there at the end of the point. The entire incident had taken at least five minutes, and both young people had seen the same thing. "I am certain of what I saw," Gregson recalled. "I returned to the golf course the next day and checked all the land formations to make sure I was not mistaken." He didn't seem to be the kind of person to make up such a story. A Grade 11 student at nearby Oak Bay High School, the boy was described by Principal John B. Wallace as a good student and certainly not a young man given to wild flights of imagination.

Almost anyone who comes face to face with an apparition finds it very frightening and young Anthony Gregson was no exception. "I believe in leaving ghosts to their own lives. I am not going back [to the golf course] again. It was an unnerving experience."

There were, of course, many other young people who were eager to search out the ghost of Golf Course Point. About the end of April 1968, 16-year-old Ann Smith was walking through the golf course with a group of school friends. Like Anthony Gregson, she noticed a sudden change in the atmosphere. It was about nine o'clock in the evening, when Smith became aware that something was happening: "There was no noise, but although it was a warm night, it began to get windy and cold near the sand pit. It was a clammy coldness."[15]

Then she saw a misty figure in the shape of a woman. It was less than five feet tall. Although the misty figure herself was not well defined, she stood out clearly from the background. There was no mist beyond the outline of the phantom.

Bravely the group decided to return to Golf Course Point the next night to see if they would encounter her again. The ghost appeared, looking much as she had the previous night and 16-year-old Dennis Andrews noticed that the figure seemed to glow. "It was about five feet tall and moved in an upright position, but I couldn't distinguish many of its features, although it looked like a woman," he reported.

"It definitely was not swamp gas," a young seaman who was with the group observed. "I know what that looks like."

As the group watched closely it became clear that the spectre was more substantial than they first supposed. "At first I thought I could see right through it," said one unidentified witness. "But after a while I realized it was opaque."

The apparition was observed by the group for about five minutes. Some of the braver members present that evening tried to get closer for a better look, but the eerie lady apparently had other ideas. "I started to walk toward her and she disappeared," Ann Smith said, "but then we turned around and she was behind us, about 20 feet away."

The late 1960s was a very active time for the Golf Course Point Ghost. A Toronto cab driver, George Drysdale, who was in Victoria during this period, accompanied his sister and some friends to the golf course one evening to see if they could find the ghost. Drysdale, at the time, was sceptical, but he was in for a surprise. In the bright moonlight, he recalled, the group could see quite well. He was the first to see the apparition of a girl. Afraid, the young man turned from her, but whatever direction he faced she would suddenly appear. "She was young and looked quite human," he said, "except for the fact that the whole outline of her body was shadowy at the edges — a very creepy effect. She looked sad — my God how sad she looked!"[16]

Drysdale's companions watched, horrified, as he tried to get away from the spectre, but he couldn't. Wherever he went it appeared in front of him. By now the young man was exceedingly frightened, because the ghost had picked him to torment, and there was simply no way to escape. Then like a flash, she was gone.

There was no doubt in Drysdale's mind about what he had seen. "A human being cannot appear in different places in the twinkling of an eye and vanish the same way," he said. "I know I saw the ghost of the murdered girl."

In the 1970s, ghostly activity at Golf Course Point almost stopped. Alarmed by the absence of the lady, the Victoria *Daily Times* sent reporter Al Forrest and photographer John McKay to investigate. Many experts on the phantom wouldn't have thought the pair had a chance of seeing anything. Most sightings were reported in early spring; this was the middle of June. The ghost was usually seen about dusk; the two men arrived at 11 PM. However, Forrest believed he saw something strange there that night. "It was a white shape, swirling in the tall grass about 15 metres from the beach," the reporter observed.[17] By the time he could train his binoculars on it, it had vanished.

A few minutes later Forrest noted a rapid change in the atmosphere where they were standing. "Suddenly it got very cold; there was a chill that cut right through me." Forrest suggested it was time to leave, but as they turned to go, the reporter noticed something. "It was very quick," he wrote later. "Like a falling star, but moved just above the grass. By the time I wheeled around and got my glasses on the spot it had vanished." The description may be quite accurate: some witnesses in the past had described the ghost as nothing more than a shapeless ball of light.

In the early 1980s, several students from the University of Victoria reported seeing the ghost at its familiar spot, and on another occasion she was reported by two people who were driving by in a car. The ghost, it seems, has returned to active duty.

Some researchers, however, have been bothered by one or two points about the golf course ghost story. First, it seems strange that she's frequently described as wearing a sheer white wedding dress. It certainly would not have been the outfit she wore to meet her husband that fatal night. Victor and Doris were hardly newlyweds. Also, why she has become so closely associated with young people is difficult to explain. After all, 30-year-old Mrs. Gravlin was no longer a teenager. The fact remains though that the Golf Course Ghost is one of Canada's most sought-after apparitions.

MORE ON THE GOLF COURSE GHOST

Certainly Doris Gravlin is one of Victoria's favourite ghosts, at least partly because she continues to haunt the place where she met her tragic death. New reports of sightings on the Victoria Golf Course in the area between Beach Drive and the sea continue to circulate.

Adding to the public's interest in this ghost is the fact that unlike most spectres, this entity is not afraid of crowds. She has appeared before dozens of astonished onlookers and, by materializing as she often does in a wispy wedding dress, seems to want to frighten people. Her gown strikes spectators as much more frightening than the clothes she was wearing the night she died.

* * * * *

During the week before Hallowe'en, the Victoria Ghost Bus Tour, sponsored by the Old Cemeteries Society,[18] has become a popular event. Indeed, these excursions to some of the city's best-known haunts are so well received that they sell out quickly and tickets must be purchased well in advance. One of the most knowledgeable guides to Victoria ghosts is historian John Adams, who came close to having his own encounter with Doris.

One evening in late October 1998, Adams waited as the passengers alighted from the bus near the pull-off by the seventh fairway of the Victoria Golf Course. Although the society has attempted to vary the haunted stops each year, it soon became clear that the Victoria Golf Course was the most popular destination and had to be included as a regular call. Because Doris is an active ghost, Adams almost always had new sightings to pass on to the tour patrons standing at the side of the road. That Doris would pay a visit during their tour seemed unlikely.

On this night, the sky was overcast and the air damp, although it was not raining. Since this was the location where Doris Gravlin had died, it seemed an appropriate place to relate her story. Adams took his usual place on the edge of the links with the clients on the sidewalk facing him. Some distance behind him were the clumps of dense bushes that bordered the green.

Adams began the ghost story. Although his audience was silhouetted against the city lights in the distance, Adams noted that they seemed distracted, shifting about nervously. Such behaviour was odd, for audiences usually stood transfixed by the tragic tale.

When he had finished the story, Adams asked his patrons to return to the bus, but no one moved. Then suddenly one of the passengers called out, "We saw her. We saw the ghost."[19]

"Yes," another person added, "she was over there." Soon the group was describing a woman in a long white dress who seemed to glide between the bushes at the side of the fairway. What was particularly strange was that her entire being seemed to shimmer. Adams, with his back to the green, had seen nothing.

Some of those on the tour said they thought the floating ghost was a hoax concocted by the Old Cemeteries Society. Adams had to explain that the society took the subject of ghosts seriously and wouldn't resort to this kind of frivolous deception.

Adams is frequently asked by tour patrons if he has ever witnessed a ghost. No, he responds, but he certainly knows many people who have seen them.

* * * * *

As was mentioned earlier, ghosts seem to have little choice about where they haunt — often the scene of their death or a place of great unhappiness — and are usually not seen very far away from that spot.

Some years ago a young couple rented an old house that they soon discovered was haunted. As is sometimes true in these cases, the couple became quite attached to the presence, even calling him "Henry." (No ghost ever materialized; only strange sounds were heard, while objects seemed to move on their own.) All was fine for a number of years, but the house was built on land zoned for apartments, and the owner eventually made plans to demolish it. The couple had to move out and they were most upset at the thought of leaving Henry. He was almost one of the family.

One day just before they were supposed to move, the couple took two chairs and sat in the laundry room. This seemed to be Henry's favourite room; he was particularly fond of playing with the ironing board. The man explained as best he could that they had to move from the house, and that they had no choice. The woman said they had purchased a house not very far away — she gave the address — and that Henry was welcome to come with them, since his house was about to be torn down, anyway. Much to their sorrow, Henry didn't go with them. As they said later, their new home was nice, but there seemed to be something missing.

* * * * *

It is easy to imagine that ghosts prefer a dusty old house full of cobwebs or isolated places like a golf course, but the evidence suggests that just about any place can be haunted. Here are a few rather unorthodox haunts.

HAUNTED HIGHWAYS

While quite common in other parts of the world — Britain, for example, has quite a number of very eerie stretches of road — so-called "haunted highways" are quite rare in Canada. British Columbia, however, has a few such roads. On the highway between Victoria and Sooke on Vancouver Island there is a spot known locally as China Flats.

Some time in the early 1940s an elderly Chinese couple homesteaded a few acres there. One day the woman was suddenly stricken ill and her husband could see she was in immediate need of a doctor. Because he didn't own a car, the farmer made his way to the highway and attempted to hitchhike a ride from a passing vehicle but none of the cars would stop and give the poor man a ride. Finally out of sheer frustration he stepped out into the middle of the highway and began waving his hands. An on-coming car struck and killed him. When authorities arrived at the farm later to break the tragic news to his wife, they found her dead.

Since then, a number of people taking the Sooke Highway have reported that a figure has suddenly darted out from the side of the road. Drivers have had to swerve immediately and jam on the brakes to avoid striking the figure. When they have gone back to the spot they have found no one there.

On at least one occasion, the hitchhiker has managed to obtain a ride. A local couple reported that while they were driving along that stretch of highway they were suddenly joined by a ghost in the back seat of their car. While the presence was not visible, both the man and the woman were convinced something had entered the rear seat of their car. What makes the story especially convincing is that at the time of the incident, the couple was not aware of the story of the Chinese hitchhiker.

Another haunted road is a section of the Upper Levels Highway, which connects Vancouver with Horseshoe Bay. A number of motorists have reported that when they reached a stretch near Cypress Creek their cars were suddenly carried along the road by some unknown force. One driver reported an apparition standing on the road, while others claim to have seen a strange red mist hanging just above the highway.

The police and highway authorities claimed the sightings were caused by natural mists, winds and even earthquakes, but Charles Yates, an authority on the history of local Indians, was more thoughtful. He noted that the Cypress Creek area was the site of a big battle between the Squamish and Haida nations many years before the coming of the white man. One may wonder if it is the spirits of dead warriors haunting that spot.

THE SIWASH CEMETERY

Haunted cemeteries are nothing new, but it is surprising when one graveyard becomes the focus of sudden ghostly activity and then, just as abruptly, all ghostly happenings cease. This was the case during the Christmas holiday season in 1940, when a number of people witnessed a ghost in the vicinity of the little Indian graveyard on Siwash Hill near Courtenay on Vancouver Island — at a place where the road passed near the cemetery and the shoreline.

What happened during the first appearance is not known, but a week later, on January 2, 1941, the spectre was seen again, this time by a logging camp mechanic, Bill Spurrill. While bicycling to work before dawn one morning, Spurrill reported seeing a "white swaying shape" across the road.[20] He brought his bicycle to a halt and watched as the shape began to assume a green glow. As he watched, it took on the outline of a human form, and then began to dissolve into nothingness.

A sceptic about such things, Spurrill ventured the notion that the ghost was caused by mist spilling over a nearby dyke and picking up the phosphorus in the sea spray. He did not explain how the mist took on human form, nor did his reasoning satisfy everybody. Another morning, while again cycling to work in the dark, he found three sailors huddled together at the bottom of the hill, terrified. They had witnessed the spectre and, as far as they were concerned, there was no natural explanation. To ensure that they would not come across it again, the trio made it clear that they weren't moving from that spot until the sun had cleared the horizon.

If Spurrill had been correct, and the ghost had been an illusion, people would probably continue to mistake the mist for something supernatural, but there were no further reports of anything unusual in the vicinity of the cemetery. The haunting stopped as suddenly as it had begun.

THE HAUNTED NIGHTCLUB

Vancouver's famous Chinatown district, like other places in this province, has played host to many strange goings-on over the years. The centre of a very active Chinatown haunting was a particularly unlikely spot — a popular nightclub known as the Mandarin Gardens at 98 East Pender Street.

The Mandarin Gardens opened its doors for the first time half way through the 1930s. This was not considered a good time to begin a business, but the owners must have believed that the public needed a place to go to forget the depression which by then had settled in across the entire country. They were right; the nightclub soon became a popular place for an evening of dining and dancing.

The mysterious occurrences began in 1938, shortly after the owner of the building, a man by the name of Chan See Wong, died suddenly at the club, and some people were convinced that the ghost was that of the late landlord. The janitor was apparently the first person to realize something was wrong. While alone in the building during the daylight hours, he heard a disembodied voice. Other staff were also aware of strange incidents. Cups would clatter, bowls would shake, and in the drawers, utensils would rattle against each other, though no one would be in the area when this kitchen cacophony began.

There were also incidents concerning the big floor-waxing machine. Much to the annoyance of the floor cleaner, the plug on the machine would be pulled out of the wall. Then, out of nowhere, the terrified employees would hear a burst of uproarious laughter, as if an unseen someone found the goings-on very funny indeed.

The activities of the ghost angered and frustrated many of the two dozen or so Mandarin Gardens staff, and the new manager, Charlie Nelson, did his best to calm their fears. As far as Nelson was concerned, the ghost was simply a product of overactive imaginations. However, one Saturday morning not long after he had taken the job at the Mandarin Gardens, his opinion about ghosts was changed abruptly.

Nelson was alone in his office working on the bank deposits when he heard something that caused a chill to run up his spine. It was the sound of a male voice, laughing. Not a pleasant sound at all, but a cold, sharp and, under the circumstances, very frightening laugh. He looked up just in time to see a hand in the doorway of the kitchen a few feet away from where he was sitting. The hand itself looked to be perfectly ordinary — except that it was disembodied. It just floated there in mid-air.

It was then, Nelson later recalled, that he began believing in ghosts. He quickly fled his office and made his way to the police station which was up the street. "I didn't run three and a half blocks because I was scared," he admitted later. "Let's just say I was a little nervous."[21] Once there he explained what had happened and then returned to the nightclub with police constable David Scotland. Together the two men searched the premises. To Nelson's consternation, there was no sign of the disembodied hand. Nor could the two men find anything else out of the ordinary. The ghost had a laugh at the expense of the embarrassed club manager, but Nelson would have the last laugh. In 1952 the building was torn down by order of Vancouver City Council. No one, of course, knows what happened to the Mandarin phantom

— the spectre with the bizarre sense of humour was never seen nor heard from again.

THE PHANTOM DANCE

Although only a few minutes by boat from the bustling Vancouver Island community of Nanaimo, Valdez Island could be a thousand miles away. The island is an example of a feature quite common in British Columbia: isolated locations which exist virtually in sight of major metropolitan areas.

In the summer of 1961, the well-known syndicated columnist, Jack Scott, and his wife were spending a pleasant summer vacation sailing among the Gulf Islands, the beautiful little islands that dot the sea between southern Vancouver Island and the mainland. The weather was ideal, and the couple's time was, with one exception, their own. The Scotts had planned a rendezvous with another couple, Gordon Graham and his wife, Lou. Graham, who was with the RCMP detachment at Ganges on Saltspring Island, was a long-time friend.

The Scotts arrived Friday, August 18, at Valdez Spit, on the southern tip of the island. The plan was to spend the weekend fishing. The Grahams weren't expected until the evening, so Scott and his wife spent the day preparing a camp. The couple selected a location a little north of the spit that seemed ideal. The spot offered good protection for small boats, and just above the high-water mark there was a grassy knoll that angled sharply up to a cliff covered in a thick growth of trees. Here they erected their heavy tent.

It was not until almost sunset that the Grahams arrived. The two couples spent an enjoyable evening sitting around the campfire watching the stars come out. About midnight, the four said goodnight and retired to bed. The fire, which had been built up during the evening, was blazing away.

Some time between two and three in the morning, Scott was awakened by a noise. As he drifted toward consciousness he realized that it was the sound of drums beating out a constant rhythm. Scott lay in his sleeping bag watching the firelight as it was projected on the canvas overhead. Curiously, he felt no fear. His natural reaction was to think that he was dreaming, but he knew he wasn't. Slowly, he rolled over on his stomach and propped himself up by his elbows. "Beyond the glowing embers I could see a great crowd of Indians dancing in the moonlight," Scott wrote later. "There was no sound from them, only the steady, muffled rhythm of drums as they moved gracefully and sinuously in and out of the perimeter of the beach fire."[22]

Scott watched the spectacle for a few minutes without feeling any alarm. He was about to wake his wife to show her the incredible sight, when Graham stirred and pulled himself out of his sleeping bag to put more wood on the fire. The fantastic dancing images then dissolved. Scott rolled over in his sleeping bag, thinking about the extraordinary display he'd just witnessed. Within minutes he had fallen fast asleep.

Hard-headed newspaperman that he was, Scott was at first reluctant to mention the incident to his wife and friends the next day. Yet the image was so real that he felt compelled to walk along the beach looking for the footprints of the dancers. There should have been hundreds of prints at the place where the Indians had danced the previous night. Of course, he found none.

Later, Graham phoned Scott from his office in Ganges. There had been a surprising development in the story. Graham informed him that two boys had found the mummified remains of a young Indian lad on Valdez Island, not far from where the two couples had camped. Also, Graham had spoken to a provincial government anthropologist in Victoria who confirmed that the area north of the spit was a Haida burial ground. "Seems there's a thousand or more Haidas buried all along the beach there, many of them victims of plague or smallpox," Graham told Scott.

The incident continued to bother Scott for some time. It was ten years before the columnist could bring himself to write about what had happened. When he finally did, he called the story "The Night I Began to Believe in Ghosts."

THE MACABRE WALKWAY

There was more than one ghost haunting the small apartment building in the Vancouver suburb of Coquitlam. Most were quite gentle presences that would do no more than occasionally let the tenants know they were around, but there was one entity that was scary.

It all started in the summer of 1985, after the owner of the apartments obtained a load of granite slabs for a walkway. One day after they were in place, a tenant, Mrs. Lucille Schneider, turned one of the stones over to discover that they were grave markers. Apparently the walkway was constructed from headstones that had been removed from graves when the Woodlands School for the mentally disabled turned its small cemetery into a park.

After that, "things" suddenly started to happen at the apartment building. The dials on the television sets in various units would constantly be changed while no one was in the room, bedroom lights would turn on and off without human intervention and mysterious footsteps would be heard to echo over the floors of empty rooms.

The ghosts did not seem to feel restricted to any one unit, but haunted the building as a whole. One particularly active presence was dubbed "Harry." "One day," reported one tenant, "I told a visitor that he would have proof soon enough [that Harry was real]. Then the toaster came on by itself and melted a plastic bread holder." On another occasion when the lights were "acting strange," she suggested that Harry should be invited for tea. "Just then, the heating element under the teapot came on."[23]

Early in the hauntings, a well-known Abbotsford psychic, Ralph Hurst, investigated Harry's activities in the apartment of Mrs. Schneider. Harry, Hurst concluded, was really a twice-married Scottish logger named Albert Johnstone who had been killed some years earlier in a work-related accident. The late Mr. Johnstone was a fun-loving sort of fellow who, according to the psychic, was a little on the lazy side. He certainly wasn't an evil individual, and he was the one responsible for the flicking of the lights and other tricks. Mrs. Schneider felt that there were other presences in the flat. At times she would catch the image of a child out of the corner of her eye, but when she turned, it was gone.

However, it was not Mrs. Schneider who was the centre of the most unpleasant manifestations, but another family, the Huttons. It started with the four Hutton children. At various times, they complained about seeing faces pressed against the window of the apartment. On other occasions, in the middle of the night, their beds would suddenly begin to shake. Mrs. Hutton could find no reason for these occurrences.

As far as the tenants of the building were concerned, the 130 little tombstones, which formed the walkway to the road, were the cause of the psychic manifestations. For children living in the building, the stones seemed to hold a macabre fascination. One of the tenants shuddered as she recalled that the local children would turn the stones over to reveal the names of the children whose graves they had marked. Finally, the tombstones were taken away, but the ghostly activity didn't stop.

It was not until December of 1986 that incidents seemed to reach a peak. Then Mrs. Hutton encountered a particularly frightening apparition outside her bathroom. "I was coming out of the kitchen and there was this figure standing there — he had a robe with red scribbling on it, but no face." The incident was very upsetting to Mrs. Hutton. "I never believed in this kind of thing — I'm not crazy," she said.[24]

The presence of the monk-like figure was the last straw. "There is no way in God's earth I am staying in this house," Mrs. Hutton affirmed. Then she quickly packed up her family and moved out. Another tenant indicated her family had endured about enough, and also threatened to move out. By then, however, the worst of the psychic phenomena were over and the number of occurrences decreased markedly over the next several months.

Today the ghosts still inhabit the Coquitlam apartment building, long-time resident Mrs. Schneider believes, but they are not nearly as active as they once were.

Haunted People

POLTERGEISTS

Poltergeists are known for their bizarre antics. During such disturbances it is common to see dishes, furniture and other household objects suddenly fly through the air and smash against a wall. The term "psychokinesis" (PK) is used by parapsychologists to mean influencing real objects without physical means. The smashing of a teacup against a wall, if it was the result of poltergeist activity, and not fraud or trickery, would be an example of PK. Although often the prime manifestation of poltergeist activity, PK is not the only kind. Poltergeist hauntings may also include the sound of ghostly footsteps, and even visible spectres.

The life of an individual who is the focus of such activity is often made miserable by the haunting. It is believed that these unfortunate people have no conscious control over the poltergeist; frequently they are unaware of their key role. The cause of the commotions is unknown, but many researchers now feel it has something to do with the release of pent-up psychic energy. The earliest recorded case of poltergeist activity in British Columbia happened 50 years ago in the little Fraser Valley town of Chilliwack.

THE THING

It became known to the residents of Chilliwack as "The Thing." There was never anything to be seen, but the noise, the loud racket it made: that was a different matter.

Anna Duryba had done well for herself. She had moved to Chilliwack from depression-hit Saskatchewan in 1933, and had worked as a domestic in a number of local houses until she could afford to buy a ten-acre chicken ranch about a mile from town. Miss Duryba's house was a four-room cottage, almost new, finished in a then-common imitation brick siding. In May 1951, Miss Duryba's 14-year-old niece, Kathleen, came from Saskatchewan to be her aunt's companion, and several months later, the strange disturbances began at the little farmhouse they shared.

It was the beginning of October when the two were first aware that something was terribly wrong. It started out as a banging sound on the northeast corner of the house. Even early on, the phenomenon was very loud — one witness described the noise as like a jack hammer striking the corner of the house. In view of the intensity of the disturbance, it seemed logical to assume that the noises were man-made.

At first Miss Duryba was convinced that the noise was created by a prankster, or maybe someone with a grudge against the family. As the disturbances continued though, she concluded that the persistent noisemaker must be motivated by something more than mischief: someone, she felt, was trying to force her to sell her property.

The difficulty was that it was impossible to catch anyone hitting the house. Moreover, the northeast wall was examined by civic authorities and there was no indication of damage. If something had struck the house with the force of a jack hammer, it should have shown on the wall, yet no marks could be found anywhere. The banging began on any of the outside walls of the house at any time of night, and what was more frightening, it moved rapidly around the house, more rapidly than was humanly possible. Worse, the dreadful cacophony would now erupt almost every night. Miss

Duryba was so upset that she began losing weight, and was often unable to sleep. Young Kathleen, too, was becoming increasingly distraught.

With the help of her uncle, Alec Duryba, who lived on the neighbouring farm, Miss Duryba set about catching the mysterious person responsible for the terrible incidents. At the height of the poltergeist activity, Mr. Duryba described the frustration involved in attempting to catch The Thing:

> We run outside when we hear it. Nothing there. Then we hear it on the other side of the house and we run around there — nothing there either. Sometimes we go in opposite directions around the house but we never see anything.[1]

The occurrences seemed designed specifically to madden and frustrate the Durybas. Miss Duryba refused to believe, even in the face of considerable evidence to the contrary, that the banging was caused by anything other than pranksters. Searchlights were brought in, while Mr. Duryba hid in the bushes with a shotgun. Neighbours, too, armed with rifles, took turns staking out the perimeter of the house, but the pounding continued.

On one occasion Mr. Duryba did have an eerie experience. "We heard it banging one night and I ... ran outside and looked around and couldn't see anything. I turned around and just then I felt a sort of wind go by me but I couldn't see anything."

There were several theories offered to explain the noises. One proposed that the thumping was the result of excessive drying of the ground under the house. British Columbia was experiencing an exceptionally long "Indian summer" and the soil was parched. The theory dissolved, however, when the fall rains finally came. The sounds continued even during the November downpours. Another theory suggested that the phenomenon was somehow related to electricity. However, the banging proved just as loud, and equally discomfiting when the power to the little cottage was turned off.

It was apparent that there was some kind of malevolent intelligence behind the happenings. On at least one occasion The

Thing seemed to know what the Durybas were asking of it. According to Miss Duryba:

> I heard him once and ran to the window. I yelled "Go ahead do it again you silly fool." Right away I heard it again — bang-bang-bang — right under the window. I was standing right there and I could see there was no one outside.

Similarly, Alec Duryba was standing outside when he challenged The Thing to perform. It did. The house shook and the window rattled right beside him but there was nothing to be seen.

The activities of The Thing were not restricted to the violent thumping on the walls. It had also thrown rocks at Miss Duryba, her uncle and her niece. By far, though, its favourite trick was thumping the walls of the little cottage. Once, a window in the dwelling was broken by the fury of the onslaught.

It was most fortunate for the Durybas that Reverend W. J. T. Clarke, pastor of Chilliwack's St. Thomas Anglican Church, was a student of psychical research. At a time when the general public knew little about them, Reverend Clarke had read extensively on poltergeists. Reverend Clarke visited the Duryba farm, interviewed the victims of the incidents, and talked with authorities involved with the investigation. In the end the minister concluded that the incident was not caused by pranksters, or even an easily explainable natural phenomenon such as electricity. No: according to Reverend Clarke, what happened at the Duryba farm was definitely supernatural.

Although scientific knowledge of poltergeists then was limited by today's standards, the minister quickly recognized that someone living in the Durybas' house was the focal point of the disturbances. The obvious choice would have been Kathleen, for it was believed that the focus for poltergeist disturbances was usually girls who had recently entered puberty.

Near the end of November 1951, Miss Duryba's niece was sent to Vancouver, both to give her a rest from the goings-on at the little chicken ranch, and to see if the incidents would stop once the girl was removed from the scene. While the disturbances decreased, they reappeared briefly on the evening of December 10, when the banging was heard for the last time. This incident, though, might have been a case of someone lending The Thing a helping hand; it was the only time during the two months that marks were found on the house.

In 1951, most scientists in North America were entirely closed minded when it came to paranormal occurrences; however, the Duryba case does appear to offer compelling evidence for the existence of poltergeists. Psychokinetic (PK) activity is often associated with the poltergeist, and in this case it was very strong: strong enough to shake an entire house. The massive blows rendered against the house, which were the prime (although not the only) manifestation of PK, could not have been done by Miss Duryba, her niece, or anyone else.

* * * * * *

Until fairly recently psychic investigators believed that poltergeist activity was almost always focussed on a young girl but according to American parapsychologist William G. Roll, this is not strictly true. Roll, in his study of 92 poltergeist cases with identifiable focal persons from 1612 to 1974, found that 61% were females, 39% males. The figures, however, tend to be somewhat misleading because the earlier data, for whatever reason, significantly favour women. Later data (1950-1974) indicate that men are as likely to be focal persons as women.

In 74 cases, where the age of the focal persons was known, it ranged from 8 to 78 years. The average age for focal males was 17 years, and for females, 15 years.

SUMMER ACTIVITY

For Clarence and Verna Walker (not their real names) of Vancouver, the sudden eruption of poltergeist activity in their home created a real problem. The Walker family attended a local church which firmly believed that such supernatural activity was the work of the devil. Both Mr. and Mrs. Walker were very uncomfortable with the strange events in their home, but it was impossible to deny what was happening.

The incidents began in the summer of 1968. The two older Walker children, Jane, 17, and Keith, 15, had summer jobs, while the two younger girls, Jill, 12, and Joyce, 10, had been at camp for two weeks. The house had been uncommonly quiet while the children were away, but the peace didn't last long. The two younger children returned home near the end of August and soon Mrs. Walker had to settle the petty squabbles that always seem to arise between children close to the same age.

One day Mrs. Walker, used to two weeks of peace and quiet, was annoyed with their constant quarrelling and decided to separate them for a while in order to give herself a respite. Joyce was duly sent to weed the flower bed in the front yard while Jill polished the furniture in the living room. Mrs. Walker saved the worst job for herself: cleaning the kitchen range. It was a hot summer day, and the front and back doors of the east-end home were wide open, though there was no breeze to cool Mrs. Walker as she scrubbed away at the encrusted oven.

Suddenly the woman was aware that the screen door at the front of the house was rattling. The noise was distinctive, as if someone had grasped the door and was shaking it. Mrs. Walker assumed it was a visitor knocking on the door, although she considered it was strange that the person did not ring the doorbell. She asked Jill, who was then in the dining room, to answer the door. In a few moments, Jill said there was no one there.

A few minutes later the screen door rattled again. This time Mrs. Walker went to the door. Nobody was there. Joyce was at the far end of the yard near the road — it would have been impossible for her to reach the door, rattle the screen and return to the flower bed before her mother got to the door. Even more mysterious, according to Joyce, no one had come through the front gate. The incident seemed strange to Mrs. Walker, but she thought no more about it and returned to her work. It was only later, when she looked back on the strange occurrences, that she decided that that was the moment everything began.

The next day Jill and Joyce were in the kitchen helping their mother make a batch of cookies. The girls were busily pressing the batter on a cookie sheet while Mrs. Walker was at the sink beginning to wash up the dirty utensils. On a counter, about halfway between where the girls were working and the sink, there was a half-filled carton of eggs. Mrs. Walker had her hands in a sink full of water when she heard a soft crushing noise. She turned in time to see the contents of one large egg run down the far wall of the kitchen.

Not surprisingly, Mrs. Walker was furious. She angrily demanded to know which girl had thrown the egg. Both, however, denied guilt. Furthermore, each girl also vouched for the innocence of the other (an extremely rare occurrence). According to the girls, the egg had moved out of its carton and hovered briefly in the air about a foot above the counter before flying against the wall and shattering. To Mrs. Walker, their story seemed entirely incredible and both girls spent the rest of the afternoon in their room.

When Mr. Walker returned from work that evening Mrs. Walker explained what had happened. He then talked to the girls but their stories remained unchanged, even in the face of losing further privileges. For the Walkers, who placed a very high value on the truth, the idea that one girl or, more likely, both, could be lying to their parents was most upsetting. But the alternative explanation — that the devil had entered their Christian home — was even worse. Mr. and Mrs. Walker were unable to decide how to deal with the situation.

Two days later Mrs. Walker and her older daughter, Jane, were sitting on a couch in the living room while the younger girls played a board game on the floor. Suddenly, a small bud vase that had been sitting on the fireplace mantel flew across the room, landing on the carpet near the opposite wall. While everyone witnessing the incident attempted to find a rational explanation for what happened, it was obvious that there was no one close enough to throw the vase. Besides, as Jane remarked later, "The vase didn't behave like it was thrown. It seemed to move too slowly — more like it was being carried."[2]

From then on the frequency of disturbances increased. Drinking glasses picked themselves up from the kitchen counter and landed on the floor; a flower vase suddenly turned over while the family looked on. The kitchen light began to flicker on and off. Walker replaced the bulb, and when that didn't work he checked the fuse and the electrical circuit. He couldn't locate the problem.

The Walkers were extremely upset by the goings-on but they refused to believe in the existence of poltergeists. Mrs. Walker, particularly, regarded the entire incident as a shame upon the family. "It was not something mother thought she could mention to our minister," Jane recalled. "In fact none of us were supposed to mention [the poltergeist] to anyone outside our family."

Fortunately, the burst of psychokinetic activity was very short. By the time school started early the following month, the disturbances had decreased, and by the end of September, they had stopped completely. While in retrospect it seems that the focal person for the poltergeist activities was either Jill or Joyce, it is not clear which it was. The poltergeist episode was one extraordinary occurrence within what was otherwise quite an ordinary family.

That Special Friend

One of the most interesting facts about the following case is the length of the poltergeist activity. While poltergeists have been reported to be active for as long as six years, most are considerably shorter. The average, as calculated by Dr. Roll, is only five months. (The Chilliwack poltergeist was active only two months; the Walker case lasted a little more than four weeks.) The next case involving Mrs. McIntyre and her son, Jason, went on for three years.

"Ghost I won't buy, but I'm willing to accept psychokinesis," Mrs. Avril McIntyre told a reporter flatly during a 1976 newspaper interview.[3]

Whatever term was applied, some of the occurrences involving Mrs. McIntyre and 3½-year-old Jason were nothing less than extraordinary. At Mrs. McIntyre's North Vancouver condominium, the unusual incidents seemed to centre around young Jason, beginning when the little boy was still a baby. "One night I found him sitting up in bed roaring with laughter — he was completely exhausted."

As Jason grew older the number of psychic experiences increased. There was something else strange as well. Jason developed an imaginary friend he called "Johnny." Of course almost all young children have imaginary friends, but Jason's was somehow different. Johnny seemed a little too close to the real thing for comfort. "For the past couple of years Jason has woken regularly at midnight and talked to Johnny until 4 AM — I've heard a grown man's voice talking to Jason. I just hide under my bed covers — what a terrible mother I must sound, but it's really scary."[4]

Jason provided a very clear description of his friend. Johnny was about six feet two inches in height with fair hair. During a time when the television serial "Daniel Boone" was important in the little boy's life, Jason described his playmate as wearing buckskins. Could it have been Jason imitating the voice of his frontier hero? Not according to Mrs. McIntyre. "There's no way [Jason] could get his voice down that low."[5]

There were other unexplained phenomena that Mrs. McIntyre observed. When Jason was about two, she recalled, "I went to his bedroom one night and found it in chaos. Bedding had been ripped, toys smashed and the legs of his bed had been torn off." Yet astonishingly, before going into Jason's room she had heard no noise at all. The young woman was extremely upset when she saw the boy's room. "I spanked him, but I regret that now," she admitted. "I realize he couldn't have caused that much damage — it takes two adults to lift his bed, let alone break the legs off."[6]

There was other evidence of Johnny's presence. A heavy fire door — much too heavy to be moved by a small child — was found standing open. There was simply no explanation for how the door was moved.

Another strange incident involved a swag lamp that was seen to move back and forth while its shade spun around rapidly. On other occasions, pictures on the wall were moved, while a decorative bottle was seen to sail across the room and hit the chesterfield. Another time the blender, which had been hanging on the kitchen wall, detached itself, and flew several feet above the floor before at last obeying the law of gravity. In each of these instances there was no one in a position to have thrown the objects. Also, cupboard doors and drawers in the kitchen would suddenly fly open for no reason.

Mrs. McIntyre and Jason were not the only witnesses to the occurrences. Friends visiting Mrs. McIntyre claimed to have seen several of the psychokinetic incidents, and a neighbour, 15-year-old Christine Foster, said she had seen the pictures move and the swag lamp sway to and fro. But there was something more frightening: she had heard weird, growling noises coming from within the house. Christine's mother, Mrs. Eileen Foster, also observed a number of strange episodes, including the moving lamp, but she was unsure whether to ascribe them to a supernatural cause or not. "I can't say yes and I can't say no," she said.[7]

Mrs. Foster also witnessed one of the strangest phenomena in the McIntyre house: the incident of the reappearing water. One day Mrs. Foster was sitting with Mrs. McIntyre and two other friends at the kitchen table when they noticed that a vase of flowers was filled with rather dirty water. What made the situation weird was that the vase contained artificial flowers, which didn't require watering. Mrs. McIntyre simply emptied the vase, but as Mrs. Foster explained, "no sooner had she returned to the table [than] the vase had water inside again." Three times Mrs. McIntyre emptied the vase, and each time it again filled with water.

Naturally, the strange events were upsetting Mrs. McIntyre. She read a number of books on the subject of psychic powers, and even bought a Ouija board. The board didn't seem to be a good idea, however. One night the wooden planchette began acting strangely: it started to move on its own all over the board — no one was touching it. By now the young woman was truly frightened and called a local priest for advice. He listened to her story patiently and then advised her to burn the board immediately. As Mrs. McIntyre soon discovered, the task was not easy. "We needed two cans of fuel in the end," she said. "The board just wouldn't burn."

The McIntyre case sparked the interest of a Vancouver clinical psychologist, Dr. Lee Pulos, and Toronto psychic researchers Dr. George Owen and his wife, Iris. What did the investigators believe was behind the Johnny phenomenon? "It has nothing to do with spirits, nothing to do with the devil," Mrs. Owen concluded. "It seems to be a way in which certain people release emotional tension."[8]

Members of the Burrard Indian band had other ideas about the manifestations at the McIntyre residence. The band chief, John George, believed that the condominium was located on or near an Indian burial ground, and that Johnny was one of his ancestors. The late Chief Dan George was also convinced that the incident was tied to Indian spirits. "You white people have hypnotism and psychic powers — well so do my ancestors," he told a reporter. "My great-grandfather could make fish appear and disappear."[9]

Mrs. Isobel Colbert, the vice-president of the Vancouver Psychic Society, was also sure that the McIntyre case was connected with local Indians. "Indians just don't like white men building on their burial grounds," she said.[10]

* * * * *

Poltergeists can be the source of considerable personal distress. No matter how daunting a haunted house may be, the occupants can always move out, but there is no such option available to someone haunted by a personal ghost. If the haunted person moves, the ghost is likely to move right along.

In some cases, though, there is nothing malevolent about a personal haunting. It is motivated by a love so great that it is able to reach beyond the grave. The following stories concern the very best of personal ghosts: those that even after death continue to love and care for the living.

SKIPPER

Frank Layard (not his real name) was six when his parents bought him a German shepherd puppy. The boy called his new friend Skipper, and for the next nine years the two were almost inseparable.

"There was no doubt Skipper was my dog," Mr. Layard later recalled. "He was like a shadow. He'd follow me everywhere."[11]

In 1945, when Frank was eleven, he and his parents moved from their home in Vancouver to a cattle ranch a few miles from Kamloops. Both the boy and the dog loved the outdoor life on the ranch. During the summer holidays Frank and Skipper would spend many hours exploring the dry, sagebrush-covered hills a few miles behind the ranch.

One of their favourite destinations was a cabin in the hills where an old man known locally as Sandy lived. "To me Sandy, with his full white beard, seemed as old as the hills. He was what I guess you'd call a hermit: he lived in a little log cabin a long way off the highway, up this narrow dirt road. But he was really a nice old man and ... our nearest neighbour."

One year, though, Frank didn't spend his summer vacation on the ranch. When he was 15, his father drove him to his grandmother's in Vancouver where the teenager was to help paint the elderly lady's house. As usual Skipper, his faithful companion, went along too.

Frank had only been at his grandmother's a couple of days when he was sent to the neighbourhood corner store to buy some groceries. On the way he held his dog by the collar, but when he reached the store he commanded Skipper to stay outside. Skipper, however, was now a ranch dog, and no longer used to the dangers of traffic. He suddenly darted out into the middle of the road where he was struck by a car. Inside the store, Frank heard the sudden squeal of brakes. "Right off, I knew what happened. It was Skipper." Frank ran outside to find his dog dead in the street.

The boy, of course, was heartbroken. "For months after the accident I would get up in the morning and expect to see Skipper there like he always was. Or on other days I'd think it was a good time to take him out for a run. Then suddenly I'd remember what happened and I'd have a sinking feeling in my stomach. And then I would start to cry."

Yet Frank increasingly experienced a feeling that Skipper was there. "I'd be lying on my bed and thinking about Skipper, about how much fun we had," Mr. Layard recalled. "And then for some reason I'd just know he was there with me. I'd look down and know he was lying beside my bed."

During the autumn of the year that Skipper died, Frank would go by himself into the hills, yet he never felt quite alone. Sometimes he would suddenly glance off to the side of the trail and catch a glimpse of a familiar sight walking along beside him. When he looked again it was gone.

Winter came early that year. After the first light snowfall of the season, Frank's father asked the boy to take a horse and ride up to make sure Sandy was set for the winter. On his way to Sandy's the boy was aware of the old familiar feeling. Even if he couldn't see the dog, Frank felt Skipper was there beside him. Sandy's cabin overlooked the narrow winding road that crossed the valley. From the distance Frank could see smoke coming out of the chimney, and hoped the old man had seen him coming and put on a fresh pot of coffee. When Frank had almost reached the old shack, Sandy came outside and greeted the boy.

"Where's your dog?" the old man asked.

"What?" Frank said, surprised. Sandy was well aware of what had happened to Skipper.

"I've been watching you and your new dog from the cabin for some time. He looks just like your old one. But where'd he go?"

Frank explained that he didn't have a new dog, but the old man was adamant. He had seen a dog following along beside the boy's horse. On the way home Frank looked at the hoof prints his horse had made on its way to Sandy's cabin. There indeed, beside the tracks in the soft snow, was a set of fresh paw prints. Frank had often seen the paw prints Skipper made in the snow and these looked the same. Stranger still, although it was impossible for a creature of that size to disappear without leaving new tracks in the snow, these paw prints appeared to do just that. The marks had come to within about a hundred yards of the cabin and then suddenly ended.

In the spring Frank's parents bought him a German shepherd puppy. Once the new dog was in the house, Frank was never again aware of the presence of his faithful friend, Skipper. "I guess when

I got the puppy, my old shepherd felt it was time to go. It was never the same, though. No dog could replace Skipper."

SOMEONE TO WATCH OVER ME

Between the time when her parents broke up in 1952, and her father remarried, Eva Roy (not her real name) lived in many different foster homes. What should have been the marvellous golden days of childhood are recalled now as only a dreary grey line of passing weeks, months and years. Yet there was one bright spot in her early life: an all-too-brief time she spent with her grandparents in Victoria. Eva particularly adored her grandfather. "After years of feeling that I didn't belong anywhere, knowing I didn't really, he taught me that I was someone special."[12] Thinking back on the few happy summer days of her childhood Eva remembered spending many fascinating hours with him by the ocean near their home. While Eva played he would sit for hours, smoking his pipe on a large boulder.

When Eva was nine, her grandfather grew ill, and it was impossible for the older couple to continue to look after an active little girl. Eva was taken off to another home. In the summer of 1964, when Eva was 14, she was living with her father and step-mother in a small town in the British Columbia interior. Eva was aware that her grandfather was very sick — she had been to Victoria to see him at Easter — but she didn't realize how ill he was. Then early one morning, about three o'clock, she suddenly awoke and found her grandfather standing beside her bed.

Calling her by a pet name he looked down at her and said, "I've got to go now ... But I'll be around if you ever need me." And then he was gone.

The next morning Eva's father broke the news to her gently, that her grandfather had passed away in the night. Eva was of course saddened, but her grandfather's early-morning visit had made it clear to her that their parting wouldn't be forever. "I knew he was there. And I knew he was saying goodbye. But it didn't seem like a separation."

Eva soon discovered what he had said was true. Whenever there was a crisis in her life, whenever she needed someone to rely upon, he would come. He would sit by her bed and smoke his pipe as he used to do when she was a little girl, and she would tell him her problems. Life continued to be difficult; Eva was often in conflict with her step-mother, but the fact that he was there to give support made the world at least bearable.

As she grew older and was more aware that the materialist world refused to accept visitations from ghosts, Eva began to doubt her own experiences. It was not that her grandfather stopped coming; he still did. It was only that Eva began to convince herself that he was no more than a product of her imagination. "I guess I thought he was something I had to comfort me: that somehow I was manifesting him, but he wasn't really there."

Something was to happen to change that. One day when she was about 20, Eva was staying at a house near the University of British Columbia. It was a particularly difficult time in her relationship with the man who would later become her husband. "I was really feeling I was at a critical point and I didn't know what to do. I remember thinking, I wish my grandfather would come."

Not long after Eva had prepared for bed she felt the comforting presence of her grandfather. He was there again, smoking his pipe and listening to her problems. When she awoke the next morning she felt better, but assumed it had all been a dream.

Then the old lady who owned the house suddenly approached her. "Who did you have in your room last night?" the woman demanded. "I heard voices."

"Maybe I was talking in my sleep or maybe it was the radio," the girl replied lamely.

"No, no," the woman chided. "It wasn't the radio. I also smelled pipe smoke."

That night was the last time Eva saw her grandfather. Today, she wants to see him more than ever, but knowing that his visits to her room were more than a product of her imagination has also made her afraid. She wonders if the fear brought about by knowing the truth about after-death survival has prevented him from ever appearing to her again.

A MESSAGE FROM THE GRAVE

The final story of this chapter concerns quite a common phenomenon: the message-bearing crisis apparition. What is particularly interesting about this case is that the message was quite literal.

When it comes to ghosts, it sometimes takes a particular incident to change a sceptic into a believer. This was the case with Andrea Lancaster who received a message from the grave. In 1985 she was living with her parents in their Maple Ridge home. It was not a particularly happy time for the family because one of her father's sisters — her Aunt Doris who lived in England — was seriously ill.

One evening Andrea had gone to bed, but had not yet fallen asleep, when she was suddenly aware of a light in her room. At first she thought that it was the reflection of a hall light in her mirror, but as she watched, fascinated, she saw that something was coming into focus. She recognized the scene before her as the cemetery near the town where her aunt lived. There in front of Andrea was the familiar family plot marked out clearly by a border of stones and shaded by an ancient oak tree. Freshly dug earth stood beside a grave. Standing there with the lower part of her body concealed in the open grave was Aunt Doris. Though her aunt had suffered terribly with a debilitating disease, the apparition before Andrea seemed miraculously restored to her previous good health.

As Andrea watched, the figure standing in the grave spoke to her. "Her voice wasn't frail or anything," Andrea recalled later. "It was just as strong as when I'd last heard it."[13]

"I want to go. I'm in so much pain," Aunt Doris said. "But I don't want to leave you or your father." After that the image slowly dissolved. The message had been perfectly clear. While her aunt was reluctant to pass on and leave her loved ones, the time was very, very near.

Three days later Andrea and her family received word from England that her father's sister had died. Aunt Doris could wait no longer.

Early British Columbia Ghost Stories

When gold was discovered in the remote Cariboo district of the colony in 1860, thousands of miners trekked into the new goldfield. (In the spring of 1862 alone, an estimated 4,000 miners made the treacherous 400-mile journey between Yale on the Fraser River and Williams Creek, site of the strike.) A number of towns sprang up quite suddenly. Most were hardly more than mining camps, but gradually some of these tent cities took on a kind of permanence. The biggest and most important of the new towns came to be known as Barkerville. Named after the miner, Billy Barker, who had struck it rich at Williams Creek in 1862, Barkerville and the surrounding mining camps grew to reach a population as high as 16,000 by the peak of the rush. As well as saloons, dance halls, hotels, stores, a newspaper and a theatre, Barkerville had its own brewery and even its own ghost or two.

THE GHOST WHO HUNG A MAN

This story of how Barkerville's famous black barber, Wellington Delaney Moses, named the murderer of a wealthy young man, Morgan Blessing, is not part of the public record. Yet the tale has been around a long time and there are many variations to the story. The first printed version dates back to the turn of the 20th century, but it was probably passed on among the miners of the Cariboo in the best oral tradition long before then.

Wellington Moses arrived in Victoria during the Fraser River gold rush in 1858 and set up a barber shop. Moses's business prospered, but with the Cariboo gold rush in full swing, Moses yearned to be a little closer to the action. He quit Victoria and opened a barber shop in Barkerville. Here too Moses prospered. Before long he added a line of women's clothes to his business.

During the extremely frigid Cariboo winters, business in Barkerville slowed, and Moses went to New Westminster to spend the coldest months of the year. It was there that the barber met Morgan Blessing. Blessing was a member of a Boston family who had come from California to seek his fortune in the Cariboo goldfields. In the spring of 1866 the two men decided to go to Barkerville together. Although they had little in common, Blessing and Moses had become quite friendly.

Unlike many who took the rugged Cariboo road, Blessing was well off and, despite Moses's warnings, the Bostonian injudiciously made no secret of this fact. In one saloon along the way Blessing paid for a couple of beers with a $20 bill. Also, he imprudently wore a large scarf pin made from a huge gold nugget. Many of those on the trail marvelled at the pin, which looked like an angel. Blessing was very proud of it, calling it his "guardian angel."

A third man joined Moses and Blessing, an American by the name of James Barry. Unlike the other two men, Barry was down on his luck to the point of being broke. A gambler by trade, the Texan boasted to his new acquaintances that he was going to hit it big in Barkerville.

At a hotel along the trail Blessing arranged for a room while his friends went to the bar. Later, when the angel scarf pin was being shown to some miners, it went missing. Barry claimed that Moses was the last man in the group to have had the object, and Blessing believed him. He begged Moses to return the angel. Many of the hotel's drunken patrons favoured lynching Moses on the spot, but the landlord intervened. Amid hoots and jeers

Moses's barber shop, Barkerville. (THE HERITAGE GROUP COLLECTION)

from the miners, the barber was ordered to leave the public house, and continued on to Barkerville alone.

Once in Barkerville, Moses resumed business. Not the kind of man to hold a grudge, he looked around town for his former friend but while he saw the gambler, Barry, often enough, there was no sign of Blessing. Barry's luck, Moses noted, seemed to have changed for the better, for now he was wearing fine clothes, and entertaining some of Barkerville's most beautiful ladies. One day Moses stopped the gambler and asked him what had happened to Blessing but Barry looked away sullenly, and would say only that he didn't know.

Several weeks later, Moses was sitting in his barber shop alone when he was surprised to see Morgan Blessing come in. Usually fastidious about his appearance, Blessing looked terrible. He had many weeks' growth of whiskers on his face and his clothes were rumpled and soiled. The man didn't speak one word to Moses but simply climbed up and sat in the barber chair. Silently, Blessing indicated he wanted his whiskers shaved off. Moses took a hot towel and wrapped it around his face. In seconds, the towel was soaked in blood. Then suddenly the apparition disappeared, leaving Moses staring at the empty chair.

Moses was sure he understood the ghost's message: Morgan Blessing was dead. Moreover, the barber was convinced he knew who the murderer was. He confided his suspicions to Chief Constable W. H. Fitzgerald, but of course, there was no evidence that a crime had been committed. It was not until September 22, 1866, that Blessing's badly decomposed body was found in a shallow grave at Beaver Pass. There was a single bullet hole in the back of his skull. Barry was tracked down and arrested. There was enough evidence to convict him; he had been foolish enough to give Blessing's angel scarf pin to a local girl.

In July 1867, James Barry was tried before British Columbia's Chief Justice, Matthew Begbie, and found guilty of the murder of Morgan Blessing. One month later, in the neighbouring town of Richfield, Barry took his last walk up the steps of the recently completed gallows; Blessing's murder was avenged.

There is a certain irony to the story, however. In an act typical of his caring nature, Moses spearheaded a public subscription drive so that the unfortunate Blessing was given a proper burial. In the end over a hundred dollars was raised — enough to ensure that Blessing's grave had a neat picket fence and proper marker. Yet when Wellington Delaney Moses died in Barkerville on January 3, 1890, no one in the community did him the equal kindness of securing a marker for his grave, and historians have been unable to trace the resting place of Barkerville's famous barber. Interestingly, the only certainty is that Moses's grave is not in the Barkerville cemetery. That ground was reserved for whites only.

THE WHITE LADY

One of the earliest ghosts to walk in Victoria was the so-called "White Lady." Her haunt was in and around the old Quadra Street

Cemetery. Who the mysterious woman was during her lifetime isn't known, but at one time her ghost was a common sight in the vicinity of the graveyard. Many a Victoria resident claimed to have seen her gliding silently between the headstones before suddenly disappearing into the earth. In the following tale, however, the lady seems to have wandered about six blocks from her usual haunt, to Langley Alley.

For the merchants of Victoria, 1861 had been an excellent year. Most of the supplies needed at the Cariboo gold-mining camps came from the island city, and Victoria wholesalers and retailers alike were prospering. On the last night of the old year it was not surprising that everyone was in a fine mood to usher in the New Year. Shortly after eight o'clock, three celebrants (their names, unfortunately, have been lost to history) decided to take a frequently used shortcut through Langley Alley, not far from the old Boomerang Inn, a favourite drinking establishment in the young city.

The trio had taken only a few steps down the alley when before them, a white shape materialized abruptly out of the shadows. The figure was that of a young woman of about medium height and rather plain in appearance. She seemed quite ordinary, perfectly solid rather than filmy in appearance, but because she was dressed entirely in white, the men took notice. They were struck by the eeriness of the white figure. As the trio watched her they were aware that she didn't step in the normal way, but instead seemed to float along as if she made no contact with the material surface of the alley. The three men were at first stunned by what they had seen. As they stared with their mouths agape, the figure crossed the alley and disappeared into the shadows at the edge.

The lady's ghostly "walk" was not over. Before the men's astonished eyes, the apparition materialized again, and crossed the alley once more — this time in the opposite direction. The trio moved quickly behind the figure and followed her until she disappeared into the deep shadows beside a carpentry shop. What was so frightening was that the figure made absolutely no sound — no one heard footfalls on the pavement or the rustle of a petticoat. The spectre gave no hint that she was aware of the three witnesses.

The incident with the Langley Alley apparition so upset one of the men that he sought out a newspaper reporter and related the story. The man also admitted that this was not the first time he had seen the woman. About eleven o'clock, two nights earlier, he had been walking along the same alley when he saw the same ghostly figure step in front of him. Her hair was very dark and hung loosely over her shoulders, the man explained to the reporter. On this occasion the spectre proceeded silently until she faded away into the blackness near a machine shop. Although at the time the figure had alarmed him greatly, he had decided to say nothing about it, for fear of ridicule. Now that his two friends had also seen the figure, he felt obliged to report what had happened.

When a Victoria paper carried the story, the reporter seemed to feel compelled to offer some kind of explanation. Rather lamely he concluded, "… some wag in the vicinity had thrown a sheet

Quadra Street Cemetery. (Photograph by the author)

over his head and perambulated the alley for the purpose of working on the fears of weak-minded persons."[1] Further, the reporter advised, the police should keep the lane under observation for future visits from the White Lady. The reporter failed to account for the fact that it was not a sheet that the three men had seen, but something that resembled a real person, save for her colour and the gliding motion when she walked.

By 1903 the lady's nocturnal walking (maybe gliding is a better word) had come to an end, and as far as is known she was seen no more. Today, the main Victoria post office stands about where the Boomerang Inn was located, and of the original Langley Alley which ran from Yates Street to Chancery Lane, nothing remains.

THE HAUNTED BED

Like most folk narratives, this tale is missing many details. Although we know the story's general location we do not know the names of the people involved or exactly when it occurred. Still, even if the facts are more than a little fuzzy it is a wonderful story.

Today, almost all the magnificent old houses of Vancouver's West End are gone. In their place, standing like tombstones for block after block, are a myriad of tall, featureless apartment buildings. However, long before one particular house fell to the wrecker's ball, something very unusual occurred there. The incident was so strange that it caused the young couple who owned the house to put it up for sale immediately.

Not long after the turn of the 20th century, a middle-aged couple moved to Vancouver and built a new house in the West End. The pair had been there less than a year when the wife suddenly died. (The woman's death was not unexpected, the husband later explained. She had had a serious heart condition.) Overcome with anguish at this terrible loss, the man quickly sold the house and moved away.

Over the next few years the dwelling changed hands several times until it was bought by a young couple for what they believed was a bargain price. Although they were generally very pleased with their home, there was one difficulty. As the couple later confided to their friends, they felt vaguely uncomfortable in it.

Months went by and the feeling continued to hang over the house. Finally, out of desperation, the couple decided to make major changes. Walls were ripped out and ceilings lowered. The entire house was repainted and new carpets were laid in most of the rooms. Their furniture was sold and new items purchased. By the time they were finished the interior of the house looked entirely different. The master bedroom, which had seemed to be at the heart of their discomfiture, was gone, replaced by a greatly enlarged drawing-room.

When the renovation was completed, the young owners decided to have a party to celebrate their "new" house. Six or seven couples were invited, and the party went well at first. The drawing-room was comfortable enough; the oppressive feeling seemed to have vanished. Then, as the new clock on the mantel counted out eleven, a hush fell over the company.

It wasn't as though anyone saw anything at first. It was simply a feeling, as if the air had suddenly become as cold as a tomb and as heavy as water. Abruptly conversation stopped and several women openly shivered. All eyes turned to one corner of the room, the area that had until recently been the master bedroom. As they watched, something was beginning to materialize out of the air.

What emerged was a gigantic four-poster bed. The image was so clear that the guests were able to tell that the huge bed was constructed of singularly magnificent rosewood. In the middle of this immense bed was the tiny figure of a woman. As she lay there, her gaze lifted until it was cast upon the blurred shape of a man sitting in an antique chair beside the bed. The shrivelled frame and sunken eyes of the bed's occupant made it apparent that the woman was only a breath away from death, but even as gravely ill as she obviously was, she still conveyed a terrible truth to everyone assembled in the room. As she looked up at the figure in the chair, her eyes were filled with pure terror.

Seconds later the image faded. The young people, naturally, were severely shaken by the incident. That night they took a pledge from their friends never to reveal what had just occurred. A few days later, all the new furniture was quickly sold at auction, and the house was put in the hands of a real estate agent.

For some reason — she was never exactly sure why — one of the guests who had been at the party decided to attend the auction of the couple's furniture, and she noticed something strange. There was the carpet that had been so recently laid in the drawing-room. It was, of course, almost new and in perfect condition, except for four deep crushes in the pile that had been made by something very heavy: something about the size of a large four-poster bed.

PHANTOM LIGHTS

Mysterious lights that appear either on the sea or on a headland have long been the stuff of sailors' superstitions the world over, and are sometimes regarded as a bad omen. Such lights are also a part of west coast lore. In one case, however, the phantom light stands not as an omen of the future, but as a reminder of the past.

On May 26, 1896, the old Point Ellice Bridge in Victoria collapsed, taking 55 men, women and children — the passengers of an ill-fated streetcar which was crossing the bridge at the time — to a watery death. Since then a mysterious red light has been reported moving along one bank of the Gorge at night, not far from where the terrible calamity occurred. The light is said to move quite slowly, about 18 inches off the ground. What the light means in relation to the tragedy is unknown.

There is also a story about a phantom light on the water somewhere off the eastern coast of Vancouver Island. Not long after the turn of the 20th century, timber cruiser Mose Ireland was working near Read Island. About two o'clock in the morning he was out alone in his boat about 75 miles northwest of Sechelt. Ireland suddenly noticed a light pierce the darkness. Then as he watched, "the light took the shape of a woman in a white robe, and it floated over the water to me."[2] Ireland, who described himself as a not overly superstitious man and a teetotaler, was frightened.

When he returned to the logging camp on Read Island, Ireland explained what had happened. Not surprisingly, among the other hard-bitten loggers, Ireland's story was received without much sympathy. They told him flatly, he was off his "reckonin'." One night when Ireland was again out in his boat, he saw the light for the second time, but in this case it was different: he had witnesses. In the boat with him were two loggers from Read Island.

It was about two o'clock in the morning and the men were rowing from Read Island to Sechelt, where they would catch a boat to Vancouver. They had reached a point about opposite Sechelt when Ireland noticed a strange cloud of light that seemed to float above the water. The bright light moved on for a while, then it suddenly changed: first sparking and then glowing with a steady white light. Then it disappeared, only to reappear again. Finally it disappeared again, and this time it did not return.

The two men travelling with the timber cruiser were clearly frightened. Ireland tried to convince them that it was a searchlight on a navy ship, but it did not behave like any searchlight the two had ever seen. Moreover, both loggers were well aware that there were no large ships anchored in the area. During the remainder of the trip, Ireland noted, neither man had much to say.

In Ireland's opinion, there was no question as to what the light meant. He was sure it was a harbinger of death or misfortune. Each time before the passing of someone close to him, he claimed to see the light. Yet, as frightening as this last incident was, Ireland couldn't help but feel a certain satisfaction in knowing he wasn't the only witness to the phantom light. "I'm an old fellow and I live alone a lot," he said later, "and people might think it fancy if I hadn't had two witnesses to back me up. It's no lie, so I'm not too ashamed to tell it."

The details of this next haunted light are sketchy at best, but the story concerned a married couple living on one of British Columbia's many small coastal islands (the name of the island has been lost). After the outbreak of the First World War, the man enlisted in the army and was soon sent overseas to battle.

When he returned a few years later he had changed greatly. It was almost as though his wife no longer knew him. The war had left its marks, but he had not suffered any physical injury; instead, he was terribly scarred emotionally.

From a man who had left home strong and robust, he was now only a shadow of what he had once been. His fear of the dark was so terrible that he carried a lantern around with him even in the daytime, just in case he might be caught without a light as darkness fell. The man's condition must have put a considerable strain on his wife, and one day, without telling anyone where she was going, she simply disappeared. Not knowing what happened to his wife, the man was frantic. He took his lantern and scoured the entire island, but she could not be found. Broken hearted, the ex-soldier soon took his own life.

From time to time after that, passing boats claimed to see a mysterious light moving about the island. As far as sailors on the coastal steamers were concerned, there was no doubt that it was the ghost of the poor ex-soldier searching the little island for his lost love.

THE TRAGIC VALENCIA

If measured only by the number of dead, the wreck of the passenger ship *Valencia* in January 1906 was not British Columbia's worst maritime disaster. When the old paddle steamer *Pacific* had gone down off Cape Flattery over 30 years earlier for example, she took with her almost twice as many victims.

However, if sheer terror is an element in disaster's equation, then the loss of the American Steamship Line vessel *Valencia* was more tragic by far. Unlike the *Pacific*, she did not slip quickly below the waves.

On January 20, 1906, the *Valencia* weighed anchor in San Francisco harbour and steamed north, bound for Seattle, via Victoria. She carried 94 passengers and a 60-member crew. At a few minutes before midnight on Monday, January 22, the *Valencia* struck a submerged reef at Pachena Bay.

High seas prevented a successful evacuation, and because the *Valencia* was wedged into the rocks close to shore, the rescue ships were unable to get close enough. They stood by helplessly while the stricken ship was pounded to pieces by the waves.

By clambering higher and higher in the ship's tangled rigging, a few survivors withstood the Pacific Ocean's onslaught for nearly two days, but in the end almost everyone was claimed by the sea. Of the 154 aboard the stricken vessel, only 37 escaped.

It was not long after the rescue ships steamed away from the scene of the tragedy that the first strange occurrence was reported. Carrying some of the survivors, the *City of Topeka* sadly made her way toward Seattle and met another ship, outward bound. The *Topeka* hove to in order to relay the news about the unfortunate *Valencia*. There was very little wind that evening and as the ship slowed, the thick black smoke from her stack settled lazily over

The Valencia. (Courtesy of Puget Sound Maritime Historical Society)

the water. Suddenly to the horror of all those present, a familiar shape emerged in the bank of curling black cloud. Displayed before them in the shifting wisps of smoke was the ghostly shape of the *Valencia*. Had the doomed ship come to pay those few survivors a final goodbye?

The *Valencia* was not ready to disappear from the waters of the North Pacific. Even years later, seamen sailing along the west coast of Vancouver Island would witness a strange phantom wreck. As they watched, the waves washed over her decks while spectral figures clung desperately to her rigging. The *Valencia*'s terrible death scene had to be repeated over and over.

There were other mysteries related to the doomed ship. During the months that followed the wreck, fishermen along the west coast would report seeing lifeboats moving over the open waters, manned by skeletons. As it turned out these tales had an uncanny resemblance to the truth.

About six months after the *Valencia* tragedy, several Indians were exploring caves in Pachena Bay, not far from where the vessel had been wrecked on the reef, when one of them happened on a lifeboat floating in one of the caves. As the man looked inside he was shocked to see, seated at the oars, a ghastly crew of eight skeletons. Like others in the area this cave was huge — 200 feet long, with a large rock partially blocking the entrance.

To get the boat into the cave, it would have been necessary to lift it over the rock. While the remains were probably those from the *Valencia*, why the occupants had gone to all the trouble of trapping themselves within the cave is a mystery. The tides in the area are very treacherous, and when others attempted to return to the spot the surging water always drove them back. The lifeboat with its grisly passengers has never been recovered.

Afterword
The Ross Bay Ghost

T he ghosts that have been described in the preceding
chapters have been otherworldly creatures as far as is
known, but the final tale of this collection is about an
apparition that doesn't quite measure up. This story takes place
in Victoria's old Ross Bay Cemetery — a location that looks as if
it should be haunted but which, strangely, has very few ghost stories
connected with it.

One Christmas Eve, some time in the 1920s, two girls were
cutting through the Ross Bay Cemetery grounds on their way
home. It wasn't late, only about seven o'clock, but even in the
daytime, the cemetery grounds always seemed rather scary.
However, as this was Christmas Eve and there was so much
excitement going on at home, the girls had more to talk about
than ghosts. They chatted on without noticing where they were.

Suddenly both girls jumped back in fear. From one of the grave
plots, they witnessed what seemed to be an apparition rise up. The
spectre was white and appeared to glow with its own light. Abruptly,
it rose in the air and floated away. The girls, needless to say, were
terrified, and they ran screaming toward the streetcar stop in front
of the cemetery, where a crowd of passengers had just alighted from

a trolley. Their story caused considerable commotion, particularly when the streetcar conductor also admitted to seeing something white floating through the graveyard.

The occurrence caused a stir in Victoria. Some city residents now refused to go anywhere near the cemetery, while members of the local psychic society maintained a lonely night-time vigil at the spot of the supposed haunting, just in case the spirit decided to pay a return visit. After a while, when nothing further happened, the group tired of the activity and gave it up, and other people forgot their fear of the old cemetery, passing by again without even a sideways glance.

The incident, however, was not entirely forgotten. Some time later, a group of people, standing in a long queue in front of one of Victoria's major theatres, began to chat amongst themselves. Eventually the discussion turned to ghosts, and one man brought up the story of the Ross Bay incident. Many in the line frankly stated their disbelief in ghosts, and made light of the girls' story. Others were less sure. Finally an elderly man stepped forward and said that the girls had been perfectly correct in their description of what they saw. He knew this for a fact because he was the Ross Bay ghost! He went on to explain what had happened.

At the time of the incident Victoria was suffering through one of the periodic recessions that marked the 1920s. With Christmas coming, and the chance of work remote, the man and his friend had hit on an idea to earn money for the holidays. One day when he had passed through the Ross Bay Cemetery, he had noted that many of the tombstones were looking shabby. As many Victoria residents were in the habit of visiting the graves of loved ones during the Christmas season, he came up with the plan of touching up the faded lettering on the graves with gold paint. All that would be necessary then would be to contact the families of the deceased and, for services rendered, "touch them up" for some cash. (The scheme, incidentally, was a huge success; the pair earned a total of more than $250.)

The pair got a list of stones to retouch, bought some expensive gold-leaf paint and went to work. The only trouble was that the work took longer than they imagined, and of course, everything had to be finished by Christmas. On Christmas Eve, armed with a flashlight, paint and brushes, as well as a couple of sheets to prevent the wind from blowing away their expensive gold paint, the men were toiling away. All was proceeding satisfactorily, when suddenly a great gust of wind picked up one of the sheets they were using as a windbreak. One man, still tangled in the other sheet, reached up to grab the first sheet, while his friend turned the light in that direction. As it escaped his grasp, he took off after it, still partially tangled in the second sheet.

The two girls happened to walk by at that moment and saw the sheets illuminated in the beam of the flashlight. The scene must have looked like something straight out of a horror film. For his part, the conductor had looked in the direction of the cemetery just in time to see the sheets blow by.

Endnotes

INTRODUCTION

1 Margaret Murray, "What I believe about Ghosts," in *A Gallery of Ghosts*, p. 20.
2 D. Scott Rogo, *An Experience of Phantoms*, p. 25.

HAUNTED HOTELS AND RESTAURANTS

1 Devon Andrew, letter, n.d. Quoted with her permission.
2 Ruth Hutchinson, letter, September 1, 1999. Quoted with her permission.
3 Personal interview with Jeanie Mathieson, June 28, 2001.
4 Joey Legate, letter, August 19, 1999. Quoted with her permission.
5 Personal interview with Lucy Wong, March 25, 2001.
6 Personal interview with Dan Hooper, March 25, 2001.
7 Personal interview with Barbara Filby, March 27, 2001.
8 Personal interview with Will Wilburn, March 25, 2001.
9 Personal interview with Lloyd Gorgerson, March 26, 2001.

A HAUNTED HERITAGE

1 Personal interview with Ruth Hoyem, December 16, 2001.
2 Telephone interview with Donna Redlick, January 4, 2002.
3 John Armstrong, *Sun*, October 31, 1987, p. H2.
4 *British Columbia: Pictorial and Biographical* (Vancouver: S. J. Clarke, 1914), I, p. 60.
5 Kim Bolan, *Sun*, October 31, 1986, p. A8.
6 Armstrong, p. H1.
7 *Ibid.*
8 Damian Inwood, *Province*, December 15, 1985, p. 10.
9 *Ibid.*, p. 3.
10 Cited in Armstrong, p. H1.
11 Personal interview with Margaret Hambrook, March 18, 1991.
12 Cited in G. E. Mortimer, *Colonist*, November 11, 1960, p. 2.

STATELY OLD HAUNTS

1 Cited in Alice Tomlinson, *Colonist*, September 23, 1979, Magazine Section, p. 15.
2 Cited in Ron Baird, *News-Herald*, February 13, 1950, p. 18.
3 J. K. Nesbitt, *News-Herald*, January 25, 1947, p. 6.
4 Cited in Baird, p. 18.
5 Cited in *ibid.*
6 Personal interview with Archie Miller, March 18, 1989.
7 Isabel Young, *Colonist*, August 23, 1979, Magazine Section p. 16.
8 Cited in Robin Skelton and Jean Kozocari, *A Gathering of Ghosts*, p. 106.

Endnotes

9 E-mail from Ann Wise to Robert Belyk, August 24, 2001.

10 James Guy Payne Audain, *Alex Dunsmuir's Dilemma* (Victoria: Sunnylane, 1964), p. 127.

11 E-mail from Stephanie Slater, Communications Manager, Royal Roads University, to Robert Belyk, January 10, 2002.

12 Personal interview with Jack Bernard, March 28, 2001.

13 *Ibid.*

14 Personal interview with Rosanna Tomkinson, March 28, 2001.

15 *Ibid.*

16 *Ibid.*

HAUNTED HOUSES

1 *Chilliwack Progress*, May 18, 1966, p. 4.

2 *Province*, May 30, 1966, p. 19, and following three quotes.

3 *Colonist*, May 31, 1966, p. 1.

4 *Sun*, June 3, 1966, p. 15.

5 *Province*, June 6, 1966, p. 1.

6 *Sun*, June 6, 1966, p. 27.

7 *Province*, June 9, 1966, p. 21.

8 *Province*, June 24, 1966, p. 10.

9 *Province*, October 3, 1972, p. 16.

10 Personal interview with Anne Houseman, March 23, 1989.

11 Margery Wighton, *Sun*, December 27, 1952, p. 18.

12 Cited in *ibid.*

13 Cited in Ernie Fedoruk, *Times*, October 31, 1969, p. 23.

14 Telephone interview with Rick Johnston, March 11, 1989.

15 Shelly Fralic, *Sun*, November 1, 1982, p. A1.

16 Telephone interview with Jim Dodds, March 12, 1990.

17 Bill Bachop, *Columbian*, May 1, 1963, p. 1.

18 Telephone interview with Angela Bremner (pseudonym), February 13, 1999.

19 Telephone interview with Ron Candy, December 6, 1989.

HAUNTED PLACES

1 Robin Skelton and Jean Kozocari, *A Gathering of Ghosts*, pp.148-49.

2 Personal interview with Joyce Watson, December 18, 1996.

3 Cited in personal interview with Alice Bishop (pseudonym), March 28, 1989.

4 Personal interview with Denny Conrad, March 28, 1989.

5 Cited in *ibid.*

6 Bishop.

7 Conrad.

8 Bishop.

9 Conrad.

10 Personal interview with Rosemary Leavitt, November 7, 1990.

11 Reby Edmond MacDonald, *Times*, September 3, 1938, Magazine Section, p. 8.

12 Telephone interview with C. J. Clark, April 19, 1989.

13 Arthur Mayse, *Colonist*, October 31, 1964, p. 13.

14 Fred Curtin, *Province*, April 6, 1964, p. 23.

15 Diane Janowski, *Colonist*, May 19, 1968, p. 24, and following three quotes.

16 Cited in Eileen Sonin, *More Canadian Ghosts*, p. 93, and following quote.

17 Al Forrest, *Times*, June 6, 1978, p. 25.

18 The organization has done much to promote public awareness of the significance of the city's historic burying grounds and the need to preserve these sites.

19 Personal interview with John Adams, June 29, 2001.

20 *Times*, January 10, 1941, p. 6.

21 Cited in Jack Wasserman, *Sun*, August 6, 1952, p. 10.

22 Jack Scott, *Sun*, August 28, 1971, p. 5.

23 Walter Melnyk, *Province*, February 21, 1986, p. 4.

24 Salim Jiwa, *Sun*, December 9, 1986, p. 3, and following quote.

HAUNTED PEOPLE

1 *Chilliwack Progress*, November 21, 1951, p. 1, and following two quotes.

2 Personal interview with Jane Walker (pseudonym), March 29, 1989, and following quote.

3 Douglas Sagi, *Sun*, December 23, 1976, p. 5, and following quote.

4 Philip Mills, *Province*, December, 23, 1976, p. 8.

5 Sagi, p. 2.

6 Mills, p. 1.

7 Mills, p. 8, and following two quotes.

8 Sagi, p. 1.

9 Mills, p. 8.

10 *Ibid*.

11 Personal interview with Frank Layard (pseudonym), October 29, 1989, and other quotes in this story.

12 Personal interview with Eva Roy (pseudonym), March 23, 1989, and other quotes in this story.

13 Personal interview with Andrea Lancaster, November 15, 1989.

EARLY BRITISH COLUMBIA GHOST STORIES

1 *British Colonist*, January 1, 1862, n.p.

2 *Province*, July 21, 1905, p. 1, and following quote.

Bibliography

BOOKS

Akrigg, G. P. V. and Helen B. Akrigg. *British Columbia Chronicle, 1847-1871*. Vancouver: Discovery Press, 1977.

Auerbach, Loyd. *ESP, Hauntings and Poltergeists: A Parapsychology Handbook*. New York: Warner Books, 1986.

Brunvand, Jan Harold. *The Vanishing Hitchhiker: American Urban Legends and Their Meanings*. New York: Norton, 1981.

Columbo, John Robert. *Mysterious Canada: Strange Sights, Extraordinary Events, and Peculiar Places*. Toronto: Doubleday, 1988.

Favourite Ghost Stories from the Tours of the Old Cemeteries Society of Victoria. Victoria: Old Cemeteries Society, 1997.

Favourite Stories from Lantern Tours in the Old Burying Ground. Victoria: Old Cemeteries Society, 1998.

Finucane, R. C. *Apparitions of the Dead: A Cultural History of Ghosts*. Buffalo, New York: Prometheus, 1984.

Forman, Joan. *Haunted East Anglia*. London: Robert Hale, 1974.

Green, Celia and Charles McCreery. *Apparitions*. London: Hamish, 1975.

Harris Lorraine. *Barkerville: The Town that Gold Built*. Surrey, British Columbia: Hancock House, 1984.

Hervey, Sheila. *Some Canadian Ghosts*. Toronto: Simon and Schuster (Pocket Books), 1973.

Higgins, D. W. *The Mystic Spring: and other Tales of Western Life*. Toronto: William Briggs, 1904.

_____. *The Passing of a Race: and more Tales of Western Life*. Toronto: William Briggs, 1905.

Leeds, Morton and Gardner Murphy. *The Paranormal and the Normal: A Historical, Philosophical, and Theoretical Perspective*. Metuchen, New Jersey: Scarecrow Press, 1980.

Lindley, Charles. *Lord Halifax's Ghost Book*. 1936; rpt. London: FontanaCollins, 1968.

MacKenzie, Andrew. *A Gallery of Ghosts*. New York: Taplinger, 1973.

_____. *Apparitions and Ghosts*. London: Arthur Baker, 1971.

_____. *Hauntings and Apparitions*. London: Heinemann, 1982.

Newell, Gordon R. *SOS North Pacific: Tales of Shipwrecks Off the Washington, British Columbia, and Alaska Coasts*. Portland, Oregon: Binfords and Morton, 1955.

Ormsby, Margaret. *British Columbia: A History*. Toronto: Macmillan, 1958.

Paterson, T. W. *British Columbia Shipwrecks*. Langley, British Columbia: Stagecoach Publishing, 1976.

Rogo, D. Scott. *An Experience of Phantoms*. Toronto: Burns and MacEachern, 1974.

_____. *The Poltergeist Experience*. Markham, Ontario: Penguin Books, 1979.

GHOSTS

Scott, Bruce. *"Breakers Ahead!": On the Graveyard of the Pacific*. Victoria: Sono Nis Press, 1982.

Skelton, Robin and Jean Kozocari. *A Gathering of Ghosts: Hauntings and Exorcisms from the Personal Casebook of Robin Skelton and Jean Kozocari*. Saskatoon: Western Producer Prairie Books, 1989.

Sonin, Eileen. *More Canadian Ghosts*. Toronto: Simon and Schuster (Pocket Books), 1974.

Wilson, Colin. *Poltergeist: A Study in Destructive Haunting*. London: New English Library, 1981.

Wolman, Benjamin B., ed. *Handbook of Parapsychology*. Toronto: Van Nostrand and Reinhold, 1977.

NEWSPAPERS

Chilliwack Progress

New Westminster *Columbian*

Vancouver News-Herald

Vancouver *Province*

Vancouver Sun

Victoria *Daily British Colonist*

Victoria Daily Times

Victoria *Times Colonist*

PERSONAL COMMUNICATION

John Adams

Devon Andrew

Jack Bernard

Alice Bishop (pseudonym)

Linda Bishop

Angela Bremner (pseudonym)

Ron Candy

C. J. Clark

Denny Conrad

Jim Dodds

Barbara Filby

M. Guibord

Lloyd Gorgerson

Anne Houseman

Margaret Hambrook

Dan Hooper

Ruth Hoyem

Ruth Hutchinson

Rick Johnston

Andrea Lancaster

Frank Layard (pseudonym)

Rosemary Leavitt

Joey Legate

Jeanie Mathieson

Archie Miller

Donna Redlick

Eva Roy (pseudonym)

Stephanie Slater

Rosanna Tomkinson

Jane Walker (pseudonym)

Joyce Watson

Will Wilburn

Ann Wise

Lucy Wong

Index

Index